Easy Electric Smoker Cookbook

EASY ELECTRIC SMOKER COOKBOOK

100 EFFORTLESS RECIPES FOR CRAVE-WORTHY BBQ

MARC GILL

ROCKRIDGE
PRESS

For general information on our other products and services or to obtain technical support, please contact our Customer Care Department within the United States at (866) 744-2665, or outside the United States at (510) 253-0500.

Rockridge Press publishes its books in a variety of electronic and print formats. Some content that appears in print may not be available in electronic books, and vice versa.

Interior and Cover Designer: Karmen Lizzul
Art Producer: Hannah Dickerson
Editor: Van Van Cleave
Production Manager: Michael Kay
Production Editor: Melissa Edeburn

Photography © 2021 Elysa Weitala, food styling by Victoria Woollard, cover; © Marija Vidal, back cover (top) and pp. II, V, 94, 162; © Hélène Dujardin, back cover (middle) and p. 42; Bauer Syndication/StockFood, back cover (bottom) and p. 16; © Darren Muir, pp. xii, 176; © Cameron Whitman/Stocksy, p. 68; © Becky Luigart-Stayner/StockFood, p. 118; © Alla Machutt/StockFood, p. 144. All icons used under license from The Noun Project. Author photo courtesy of Jonathan Greye.

ISBN: Print 978-1-64739-633-6 | eBook 978-1-64739-634-3

R0

To my
beautiful grilling
partner, Trish.
A very special thank you
to Gus Ibrahim,
Scott Meadow, and my
friends on FB&YT.
You rock bros!

Poultry Rub,
page 164

CONTENTS

INTRODUCTION

've spent a big part of my life cooking outdoors. In fact, I host a social media channel, Marc's on the Grill! (Find it on Facebook, Instagram, and YouTube: @MarcsOnTheGrill.) The channel is dedicated to testing out new grills, smokers, fryers, and any other fun equipment for cooking up something totally awesome and over the top.

Although grilling and smoking food the traditional way, with offset and barrel smokers, brought me delicious results, I didn't like how much time it took. Standing over an old-school smoker, tending the meat every few minutes and manually adjusting temperatures, doesn't give you a whole lotta time to enjoy the things that make life worthwhile. And if you want to grill or smoke in the winter in a snowy climate, you better have a good shovel!

Thirteen years ago, I was invited to work on the original model of the Big Easy, an oilless turkey fryer from Char-Broil that evolved into the "3-in-1" Smoker-Roaster-Grill of the early 2010s. The grill was getting mundane, and the smokers were getting easier. I was ready to dive deeper into smoking.

Then, in 2012, my work as a TV chef led me to the gold standard of smokers at the time: the Masterbuilt. This great machine made it easy to get tasty smoked food without the babysitting and mess. Critically, it had easy temperature control. Finally, I could relax while smoking, and I could even do it in cold weather. I've never looked back.

Electric smoking is satisfying (and addictive!) because it makes "set-and-forget" cooking a reality. It has truly revolutionized the way we barbecue. All you have to do is season your food, add the wood, and press some buttons, and your smoker will cook your food to perfection by itself. The electric smoker is the great equalizer: Novices can easily do what competition pitmasters do. Bacon-wrapped pork heaven for all! I call the trailer for my offset smoker my "party on wheels," because it allows me to hang with my friends and family while making them dinner. After all, good barbecue is about bringing people together.

Ease, authenticity, and deliciousness are the foundations on which this book is built. Many delectable morsels are in your future, with recipes for poultry, pork, beef, fish, shellfish, vegetables, sides, cheese, nuts, marinades, rubs, and sauces, not to mention food that you never thought about smoking before. Smoked Pineapple Chocolate Upside-Down Cake (page 160), anyone? I've covered the must-haves, like Smoked Beef Brisket (page 70) and 3-2-1 Smoked Ribs (page 46). And because other cultures have their own claims to BBQ fame, I've added a few internationally inspired favorites, like Korean-Style Short Ribs (page 80) and Pernil-Style Smoked Pork (page 62).

I encourage you to make these recipes your own. Get creative and try different woods and spices or experiment with brines and marinades. I'll give you some guidance on how to mix and match your recipes in chapter 1, but for now, there are just two rules I want to leave you with: First, always watch your temperature and time. Lucky for you, with new electric smoking technology, that's never been easier. And second, there are no rules! Smoking is all about having fun and experimenting, so roll up your sleeves, grab a beer, and I'll see you out back!

Set-and-Forget Smoking

F YOU'RE LOOKING FOR MOUTHWATERING, smoky flavor without spending all your time tending a fire, you're in the right place. Yes, this book is about getting the best results out of your electric smoker, but, even more than that, it's about spending time with family and making time for friends.

On this journey, I'll tell you why I think electric smoking is the ideal set-and-forget barbecue method and what you need to know about using and caring for your electric smoker. I'll also let you know what tools and ingredients I always have on hand. When it comes to wood, I'll show you my favorites and explain what makes them unique, so you can learn to use them like the special spices they are. Finally, I'll give you some ideas for serving some memorable meals. Whether it's a casual dinner with friends, a family reunion, or a spectacular holiday meal, you'll find your inspiration here.

HOW SMOKING WORKS

First and foremost, smoking food is all about burning wood. Wood contains a substance called cellulose, and when the cellulose burns off, it releases sugars and vapors that build the colors and tastes we associate with smoking. Each type of wood has different minerals, oils, and moisture levels that give off unique flavors. Various particles and oils in the smoke can affect the sweetness or bitterness, while the level of moisture in the wood plays a big role in whether the food has a light or heavy smoky flavor. Additionally, the heat level can affect how much of that "wood flavor" is imparted to the food. All these factors contribute to the otherworldly smells and tastes of smoking. You know that tipsy, "holy moly, that's good!" feeling you get when the smell of smoked meat wafts into your nose? That's what I want you to experience every time you use your smoker.

Before we dive into specifics, let's talk about what kinds of meats smoking works best for and what types of smokers you can choose from. First, for low-and-slow smoking, beef and pork are your best bets. Some cuts of beef, like brisket or ribs, need that long process to tenderize the meat and build up the crust, or "bark," where all the flavor is concentrated. Other cuts, like tenderloin and steaks, smoke more quickly. Chicken, turkey, and duck are all smoker-friendly and pair particularly nicely with a fruity or light wood. Fatty fish such as salmon or firm fish like tuna or grouper pick up great flavors from the smoke. Shellfish smokes quickly, so it can be wonderful for appetizers or as a main course. For a stand-out snack or after-dinner treat, nuts and cheese, when smoked at low temperatures, are crazy-good.

When it comes to choosing an electric smoker, the differences between models come down to quality, versatility, and product support. To start, consider your budget and how much food you want to smoke on average; also take the time to read reviews and get trusted referrals. At the end of the book, I list some great resources for the best electric smokers out there.

Beyond that, you should know the difference between the two main types of electric smokers so you can choose the model that best suits your needs. Chest-style electric smokers are vertical boxes with multiple racks. They use chips and have been designed specifically for low-and-slow smoking. Bradley and Masterbuilt are two of the best-known makers of chest-style electric smokers. Pellet smokers, on the other hand, are newer to the market and getting more popular every year. That's because they can reach higher temperatures than chest-style smokers and are therefore much more versatile, like an outdoor oven that gives food smoky flavors. Rec Teq makes superb pellet smokers with high-grade stainless steel, has engineered one of the best temperature controls in the market, and has excellent customer service teams. With the pellet smokers from Green Mountain Grills, you can add some special features, including a pizza attachment—reason enough to get this smoker.

Why Go Electric?

Smoking food is an ancient cooking tradition that has been used all over the world. Until refrigerators were invented, most meat was brined, seasoned with basic salts, spices, and herbs, and smoked over an open fire. Then in the 20th century, North Americans started smoking more to experience the flavor than to preserve the food. Amazing smoking recipes were developed all around the world (more on that later), while the American BBQ Belt popularized the "low-and-slow" smoking style of the early offset smokers.

More than 30 years ago, Traeger came out with the first electric pellet smokers. They used an auger, which was basically a long screw, to move hardwood pellets of a uniform size and moisture into a box. This box was fired by an electric element with a fan to keep the smoke moving over a horizontal, barrel-type smoke box. These electric pellet smokers have proliferated like crazy because they have made smoking basically effortless.

One of the main reasons to use electric smokers is their versatility. If you want to smoke at a cooler temperature, you can open the air vents. On the other side of the dial, you can get pellet smokers to over 500°F and some brands will take you over 700°F. That means you can get a good sear on a steak or a chop and then be able to dial it down to a lower temperature for a richer, smokier taste. That higher temperature range also lets you make desserts. If you haven't tried making a cheesecake or other cakes in a smoker, you don't know what you've been missing!

Another reason you'll be happy with electric smokers is the consistency in their results. Today, you'll find electric smokers with apps to help you cook the food you want, just the way you want it. With sensors for the internal food temperature and controls for the smoke, you can be sure of your food's level of doneness, whether it's a 16-hour smoke for a 12-pound pork butt or a quick and hot one for a rib eye. On top of all that, electric smokers are a lot cleaner than the old locomotive types, and—as long as you clean the grease pan—much safer to use.

YOU CAN SMOKE THAT?!

Everyone knows about smoked beef, pork, and poultry. But there are so many more types of food that you can smoke. For starters, consider this treasure trove of smoked food:

 Cheese: With a low temperature and little time, you can smoke cheese for a fantastic snack, dip, spread, or salad. Cheddar and Gouda are the usual suspects for smoking, but smoked Parmesan takes it to the next level of flavor. You can also try soft cheeses like mozzarella, Monterey Jack, Brie, and Gruyère.

 Desserts: There are so many desserts you can make in an electric smoker, no kidding! Because the pellet smokers reach higher temperatures, you can bake cakes with hints of smoke that add a special flavor.

 Eggs: If you've never tried a smoked egg before, you'll be pleasantly surprised by their complex flavors; try Smoked Deviled Eggs (page 154).

Nuts: After dinner or as a snack, smoked nuts are crave-worthy. Make them sweet, salty, or spicy—or all three!

 Sauces: Think sauces are just for after the smoking? Think again. Giving BBQ sauces, and even ketchup, the smoke treatment makes basting and dipping more fun and flavorful.

Seafood: We've all tasted smoked salmon, but what about smoked grouper or lobster? With just a little brining or spicing, firm-fleshed fish and all kinds of shellfish go from everyday, ho-hum dishes to unbelievable explosions of smoky goodness on your plate. Shrimp, lobster, oysters, and clams also come out great after a smoky bath.

HOW TO USE YOUR ELECTRIC SMOKER

This section describes the features of your appliance, as well as steps to get you started smoking.

Parts of the Smoker

Chest-style smokers use wood chips and have a max temperature of 275°F, while pellet smokers use hardwood pellets and can reach up to 550°F or higher.

Chest-Style Electric Smoker Parts

AIR DAMPER: Controls the flow of air into and out of the smoker

CONTROL PANEL: Sets temperature and timing for the cook; works with the remote control or app

COOKING RACKS/SMOKER RACKS: Removable shelves that hold the food for smoking

DOOR: Gives access to the smoker box

DRIP PAN: Captures the drippings from the food

ELECTRIC ELEMENT: Heats the wood chips to the desired temperature

GREASE TRAY: Collects the grease from cooking

REMOTE CONTROL: Lets you monitor and control the cooking remotely

SMOKER BOX: The main chamber where the food is smoked

WATER PAN: Provides moisture to the food being smoked

WOOD CHIP LOADER: The part that adds fuel, i.e., wood chips, to the wood tray

WOOD TRAY: The place where the chips fall and are heated to produce smoke

ASH CUP: Collects the ashes falling from the burn box

AUGER ASSEMBLY: Delivers fuel from the pellet hopper to the burn box

BUCKET: The source of fuel for the pellet smoker

BURN BOX: Where the combustion of pellets takes place

CONTROLS: To set temperatures and time for smoking

FAN: Blows the smoke through the firebox

FIREBOX: The chamber where the food is placed for cooking; accompanied by lids

FOOD PROBES: Devices inserted into the food to check internal temperature

GRATES: Metal grills inside the firebox used for smoking or searing meat

GREASE BUCKET: Collects the drippings and grease from cooking

HOPPER: Feeds the pellets into the auger

IGNITER: Starts the burning of the pellets

RACKS: Provide space for additional cooking; located above the grates

REMOTE CONTROL: Supports Bluetooth and Wi-Fi connections to "set-and-forget"

SMOKESTACK: The tube attached to the firebox where most of the smoke leaves

Smoking 101

Now you're almost ready to get smoking! Here are step-by-step instructions on how to use your chest-style or pellet electric smoker. This section is critical to the well-being of you and your smoker, so don't skip it!

Chest-Style Electric Smokers

1. If your smoker is new, season it before the first use. To do this, set it to the maximum temperature for 3 hours. In the last 45 minutes, add 1 cup of soaked wood chips to the loader. Let the smoker cool down and then wipe the inside with a clean cloth.

2. After seasoning the smoker, soak the wood chips for about 30 minutes.

3. Load the wood chips according to the manufacturer's instructions.

4. Preheat the smoker to its highest temperature. Let it preheat for about 35 minutes before you put the food on the racks.

5. Add the food, leaving space between different items. This makes sure that the food will cook evenly and be evenly flavored.

6. If you're using an app or remote control, enter the information about the type of food and weight. If not, refer to the specific recipe. Set the smoker to your time and temperature. If the cook time is over 1 hour, you may need to add more chips. When you do so, be careful because the loader will be very hot.

7. Remove your food and turn off your smoker. After each use, clean the smoker with soap and water to remove grease and oil (once it has cooled down). Also remove the ash and residue from the wood tray.

Pellet Electric Smokers

1. Before your first cook, you need to "prime" and season your smoker. To prime your smoker, fill the hopper with wood pellets. Take all the shelves and racks out. Set your smoker to its lowest temperature. After a few minutes, you'll hear the pellets falling from the auger tube into the burn box. At this point, shut down the smoker. To season the smoker, set the

temperature to low and wait until it's preheated; you'll see smoke coming out of the smokestack. Run it for about 30 minutes and then shut it down. Most pellet smokers have a shutdown phase that prepares the smoker for the next cook.

2. When you're ready to smoke, add the pellets to the hopper.

3. Set the temperature. If you're using an app that came with the smoker, enter the type of food, weight, and any other settings that are required. If not, refer to your recipe.

4. Start cooking, monitoring the time your food has been in the smoker.

5. When you're done cooking, shut down the smoker and retrieve your food. When it's cool, be sure to clean the probes and sensors.

TOOLS FOR SUCCESSFUL SMOKING

To ensure smoking success, it's important to have the right pantry staples and equipment on hand. In this section, I will walk you through my favorites.

Pantry and Fridge Staples

APPLE JUICE: For caramelizing meat

BLACK PEPPER: For brines, marinades, and rubs

BROWN SUGAR: For beef and pork rubs

BUTTER: For frying, stuffing under the skin of turkeys, and basting

CAYENNE PEPPER: For spiciness

DRIED HERBS AND SPICES (SUCH AS CUMIN, CILANTRO, AND THYME): For building unique flavors

GARLIC (POWDERED, GRANULATED, AND FRESH): For brines, marinades, and rubs

KETCHUP: For sauces

LEMON ZEST: For freshness

MOLASSES: For sauces

MUSTARD: For coating meat to help rubs stick

OLIVE OIL: For coating meat to help rubs and other spices stick, for frying, and for marinades

ONION (POWDERED, GRANULATED, AND FRESH): For brines, marinades, and rubs

PAPRIKA (SWEET, SMOKED, AND HOT): For brines, marinades, and rubs

RED PEPPER FLAKES: For spiciness

SALT: Coarse for brining and rubbing; kosher salt or coarse sea salt are the best

SESAME OIL: For adding additional flavor in Asian-inspired recipes

TOMATO SAUCE: For BBQ sauce

WORCESTERSHIRE SAUCE: For sauces

Accessories

There's no lack of gadgets for smoking. Some are absolutely essential, and others are just nice to have. Here's a list:

DISPOSABLE GLOVES: Go get a box of these because you'll go through them fast. You need gloves to handle raw meat. It's the only way to be really safe.

GRILL SCREENS, GRILL MATS, AND COOLING RACKS: Wire-mesh screens, solid grill mats, and standard kitchen cooling racks are all incredibly useful for food that might fall through the spaces on the smoker's grate or cooking rack. They're good up to 500°F.

LONG-HANDLED BRUSH: Get a stainless steel brush with a good scraper. This will help you keep your smoker clean, so you stay healthy and safe.

LONG-HANDLED METAL TOOLS: You definitely need a set of tough tools, including spatulas, forks, and tongs, which are great for turning sausages, chicken, ribs, and brisket.

OVEN MITTS: Everyone, and I mean everyone, needs a good oven mitt because it's hot by the fire. You can get BBQ mitts made with quilted cotton or leather gloves with extensions that will make you look like a gladiator. With a good set of silicone mitts, you can safely handle smoked food, smoker racks, hot pots and pans, and utensils.

PERFORATED BBQ SKILLET: If you want to smoke veggies, fish, or shrimp and you don't want to use a skewer, use a perforated BBQ skillet (ideally nonstick). The holes are big enough to let the smoke flow over every morsel and but small enough that nothing falls through the grates.

SKEWERS: If you want to make kebabs, you will need skewers. Flat metal skewers make it easy to keep the food in place. The best ones have double tines so that the food doesn't spin around. They also have "pushers" that help slide the food easily off the tines. Be sure the handles are long enough to keep you from cooking your hands as well as your food. You can also use wooden skewers, but remember that they need to be soaked in water for at least 30 minutes before cooking.

THERMOMETERS: There are some great digital thermometers on the market that let you get near-instant reads on the temperature of your meat and poultry. The good ones have heatproof leads that let you monitor the temperature without having to open the grill cover. If your grill doesn't have a thermometer, you can get one that attaches magnetically to the grill rack.

OTHER STUFF: Have a roll of butcher paper or aluminum foil on hand to wrap meat for some low-and-slow recipes. Keep a spray bottle around for spritzing the meat with liquid when it's being smoked. And, occasionally, you may want to have a marinade injector (see Argentine-Style Smoked Boston Butt, page 48).

Navigating the Woods

When we looked at the science of smoking, I explained why different wood gives a different taste. Some people like it stronger and some want a lighter touch. Here's a guide to 10 of what I think are the best woods for smoking. Some of the lighter and fruitier woods can be fortified with the stronger ones to give a unique flavor. You can buy premade mixtures, too.

WOOD	FLAVOR CHARACTERISTICS	WHAT TO COOK WITH IT
Alder	Very light and delicate smoke	Salmon, poultry
Apple	Mild and sweet; takes time for the smoke flavor to set	Chicken, turkey, pork, cheese
Beechnut	Has the nuttiest flavor of all the woods listed	Beef, pork, poultry, vegetables, nuts, cheese
Cherry	Sweet and mild; mixes wonderfully with hickory	Poultry, pork, venison, cheese

WOOD	FLAVOR CHARACTERISTICS	WHAT TO COOK WITH IT
Hickory	A heavy smoke that's still sweet with a little hint of bacon; too much will make the food bitter	Beef, ribs, pork, chicken, turkey, nuts, cheese
Maple	Very light, mild smoke that's also sweet	Poultry, pork, duck, cheese
Mesquite	Intense, strong, woody smoke; leaves a deep reddish-brown color	Beef
Oak	Not too heavy, not too light—a nice medium-level smoke	Sausages, brisket, beef, cheese
Orange	Mild with a smoky flavor	Any meat
Peach	Like hickory, but sweeter and milder	Pork, poultry
Pecan	Very sweet and nutty; good to mix with other woods	Beef, ribs, cheese

'CUE YOUR CREATIVITY

Use this book as an inspiration for your own creations. Adjust the recipes for rubs, seasonings, sauces, and marinades to your tastes and make up your own. Try out different woods. Just remember to follow this book's basic guidance on matters like brining and marinating times. You'll find the Smoke Time Cheat Sheet (page 178) especially helpful.

SAFETY, TROUBLESHOOTING, AND MAINTENANCE OF ELECTRIC SMOKERS

Maintaining your smoker may not be the most exciting part of your smoking experience, but it does make the cooking process safe and effortless. Some brands are more reliable than others, so read several reviews before you buy one and ask your friends, too. When it comes to troubleshooting, it's best to know the manufacturer has your back with good customer service. And it's important that you read the manual that comes with your smoker and then hold on to it for future reference.

Safety

For me, cooking outdoors is all about family, friends, and fun. And that means you have to keep it safe, too. Below are my tips for safe smoking.

→ First, remember that outdoor cooking means *outdoors*. Don't smoke in the house or in the garage.

→ Keep a fire extinguisher on hand, just in case.

→ Watch out for the hot surfaces of smokers, and likewise, be careful with the grills and grates. The handles are there for a good reason.

→ It's a good idea to use silicone BBQ mitts, because not everyone has tough-as-leather chef's hands.

→ If it's raining, it's better to not use the electric smoker, unless it is well protected under an awning or a BBQ tent of some kind and it's plugged into a safe, dry outlet, which must be grounded.

→ If you're using an extension cord, make sure it can handle the electric current that the smoker requires and that the connection's dry.

→ And again, read the safety instructions in the owner's manual.

Troubleshooting

"Stuff happens," so here are a few tips on fixing the most common issues with electric smokers. As a warning, pellet smokers have more moving parts than chest-style smokers—including augers, fans, and igniters—so there may be more troubleshooting to do with them. (But I love them anyway.)

→ If the smoker doesn't turn on and it's plugged in, check all the connections. If they're okay, check the fuse in the breaker box.

→ What, no smoke? Check to see that you haven't used up the chips or pellets.

→ If the smoker heats and then keeps going off, check to see that the thermostat is clean.

→ If the temperature display shows that the smoker is on, but there's no heat, then something's wrong with the controls. Call the customer service number in the owner's manual.

→ If you have a pellet smoker, the auger may get jammed. That's usually because pellets were left in the auger and they got too moist. Unplug the smoker and remove them by hand. If the auger still doesn't work, call customer service.

→ If you have a pellet smoker and the auger is feeding the pellets into the burn box but there's no ignition, you're going to have to replace the igniter.

→ If you see the temperature go up quickly on a chest-style smoker, that doesn't mean that you have to fiddle with the temperature controls. It will level out in a few minutes.

Maintenance

You'll get a lot more life out of your smoker if you maintain it properly. To give it some TLC, follow these steps:

1. Clean the drip tray or pan and empty the ash cup after each cook.

2. Remove any unused chips or pellets after each cook.

3. Use a good brush to clean the grates and racks.

4. Scrape any soot or buildup off the interior.

5. Wash the smoker down, inside and out, with warm, soapy water. Make sure you clean off the thermostat and any other sensors.

6. Keep the smoker unplugged and covered when you're not using it.

BARBECUE SLANG

So you feel like a real pro, I've put together a list of BBQ slang that you can toss around while you're hangin' with your buds. Now you'll really commit to the flip!

3-2-1 ribs: This is the classic way to make ribs where you smoke them for 3 hours at a low temp, wrap them in foil and continue cooking for another 2 hours, and then unwrap them for a final hour at higher heat while basting them. We have the recipe right here (page 46) in this book for ya!

Bark: Mmmmm, arguably the best part of the beast, the bark is the crusty outer layer of concentrated flavor on a brisket or other type of smoked meat.

Blue smoke: When the smoke turns blue, that'll do! Blue smoke is when the smoke is tinged slightly blue because it's so hot. It's the best time to slap the meat on your smoker!

Jiggle: If the brisket has a nice jiggle to it when you touch it, it's done!

Low and slow: Low heat and lots of time for tender meat–that's low and slow.

Money muscle: In BBQ contests, it's the piece of pork–the high point on the shoulder, which is very moist and flavorful–that usually takes home the cash.

Reverse sear: After you've cooked meat for a long duration over low heat, you finish it off with a nice sear over high, direct heat to get that nice crisp we're all looking for.

Texas crutch: This is when you wrap meat in aluminum foil after the meat has taken in a good amount of smoke, but still isn't totally cooked yet. This preserves moisture while it finishes cooking.

The stall: This is when the temperature of smoking meat plateaus or falls even though it hasn't come to the ideal temperature.

PLAN A COOKOUT

Now, when you're smoking, you're not playing solitaire. Cuein' is about having fun and enjoying great food with family and friends. So, here are a few tips for hosting get-togethers that will delight your guests and show off that great smoker in your backyard.

→ First, it's important to have all the ingredients lined up and ready—after all, you are part of the show!

→ Time and temperature are the most important parts of making a cookout a memorable experience. So, be sure that you plan for low-and-slow cooks and line up the recipes to prepare ahead of time.

→ You'll want to be sure to serve desserts right after they come out of the smoker.

Casual BBQ with Friends

Snack on Smoked Almonds (page 150) and Smoked Candied Nuts (page 151) while you're waiting for the Pulled Pork Sandwiches (page 47) and Smoked Mac 'n' Cheese (page 120) to finish. To drink, there's nothing like cracking open a cold, crisp beer to go with this laid-back lunch or dinner. It's even better if someone else brought it.

Family Reunion

Try Smoked Turkey (page 20) served with Bacon-Wrapped Asparagus (page 124) and Smoked Pineapple Chocolate Upside-Down Cake (page 160) for dessert. After dinner, serve Smoked Almonds (page 150) and Smoked Cheddar Cheese (page 147). An oaky white wine like chardonnay goes well with the turkey.

Holiday "Smoketacular"

For starters, serve Bacon-Wrapped Smoked Scallops (page 98). Then wow your guests with Bacon-Wrapped Beef Tenderloin (page 82) and Smoked Vegetable Casserole on the side (page 129). Basque-Style Cheesecake (page 158) makes a great smoked dessert. Try a big red wine like a syrah to go with the beef. A glass of port wine or cream sherry is a nice endnote after the cheesecake.

Jerked Chicken,
page 36

Chapter 2

Poultry

WHEN IT COMES TO POULTRY, you have a lot of choices, from chicken and turkey to duck and Cornish hens. Smoked poultry is excellent for any occasion, whether everyday meals or big holiday feasts. In this chapter, you'll discover my own takes on recipes that my family, friends, and I love from all parts of the USA, as well as from the Caribbean, Latin America, and Asia. A couple reminders before you get started: First, be sure to use an instant-read food thermometer. And second, though poultry gets much of its flavor from brining and marinating, be sure not to let it soak for too long or it can get stringy. Ready to get your smoke on? Let's light it up!

Spicy Smoked Chicken Wings

SERVES 4

PREP TIME:
1 hour

SMOKING TIME:
1 hour
30 minutes

TEMPERATURE:
250°F
and 425°F

WOOD:
Cherry

Wings are a classic backyard favorite for a laid-back meal with family and friends. These crispy, spicy wings are irresistibly flavorful, so I suggest that you make a lot of them. Serve the wings with your favorite dressing—such as ranch, blue cheese, or Thousand Island—along with carrot sticks and celery.

32 chicken wingettes (flats) or 16 whole wings cut in half at the joint

1½ cups all-purpose flour

½ cup Poultry Rub (page 164)

½ cup hot sauce

½ cup store-bought barbecue sauce or Bacon-Flavored BBQ Sauce (page 170)

1. Pat the wings dry with paper towels.

2. Put the flour in a shallow bowl and mix in the rub. Coat the wings in the mixture, a few at a time, then place them on a sheet pan.

3. Refrigerate the wings, uncovered, for about 45 minutes. The air in the fridge dries them a little, which will make them extra-crispy.

4. Preheat the smoker to 250°F.

5. Smoke the wings for 30 minutes.

6. Take them out and increase the temperature of a pellet smoker to 425°F (if you don't have a pellet smoker, finish the wings in the oven). Place the wings in a bowl and douse them with the hot sauce and barbecue sauce.

7. Return the wings to the smoker and smoke for 1 hour, or until their internal temperature reaches 165°F. Serve the wings warm.

Smoked Spatchcocked Turkey

SERVES 8

PREP TIME:
1 day

SMOKING TIME:
6 hours

TEMPERATURE:
225°F

WOOD:
Hickory mixed
with alder or
beechnut

When you spatchcock a turkey to smoke it, the dark and white meat get done at the same time and all the turkey skin gets crispy. This is a great dish for celebrations with your family and friends. To cut down on the prep time, ask your butcher to spatchcock the turkey.

1 (12-pound) whole turkey

¼ cup coarse salt

2 tablespoons dried rosemary

¼ cup Poultry Rub (page 164)

1. To spatchcock the turkey, place the bird breast-side down on a large cutting board. Use poultry shears to cut along both sides of the backbone from front to back. Remove the backbone. Turn the bird over and press firmly on the breast with the heels of your hands until it cracks to flatten out the turkey.

2. One day before smoking, dry-brine the turkey. Place it skin-side up and rub with the salt. Where possible, rub the salt under the skin and in the cavity. Place the turkey in a plastic bag or wrap it in plastic wrap. Refrigerate it overnight.

3. When you're ready to cook the turkey, preheat the smoker to 225°F.

4. Rinse the salt off the turkey. In a small bowl, mix together the rosemary and poultry rub. Generously spread the mixture all over the turkey.

5. Smoke the turkey for 6 hours, or until the internal temperature in the thickest part of the thigh reaches 165°F.

6. Let the turkey rest for 15 minutes before carving.

KNOW YOUR INGREDIENTS: If you want an extra spicy "zing" to the turkey, add 2 teaspoons of red pepper flakes to the rub.

Smoked Turkey

SERVES 10

PREP TIME:
12 hours

SMOKING TIME:
8 hours

TEMPERATURE:
225°F

WOOD:
Maple

Why wait for Thanksgiving for a fabulous smoked turkey? It's delicious any time of year! The buttermilk brine brings the spices deep into the meat for an unforgettable flavor.

FOR THE BRINE

1½ gallons cold water, divided

1 cup coarse salt

1 cup packed light brown sugar

2 lemons, sliced

2 tablespoons black peppercorns

2 tablespoons coriander seeds

2 tablespoons yellow mustard seeds

2 tablespoons onion powder

1 tablespoon ground cumin

1 tablespoon paprika

1 tablespoon dried sage

4 thyme sprigs

4 bay leaves

¼ cup minced garlic

1 gallon buttermilk

FOR THE BIRD

1 (14- to 16-pound) whole turkey

4 tablespoons (½ stick) unsalted butter, at room temperature

2 tablespoons salt

2 tablespoons freshly ground black pepper

2 tablespoons granulated garlic

TO MAKE THE BRINE

1. In a large pot, combine 1 gallon water, the salt, brown sugar, lemons, peppercorns, coriander seeds, mustard seeds, onion powder, cumin, paprika, sage, thyme, bay leaves, and garlic. Place the pot over medium heat and cook until the sugar and salt dissolve.

2. Remove the pot from the heat. Add ice or place it in the refrigerator to cool. When completely cool, add the remaining ½ gallon water and the buttermilk.

3. Line a large bucket with a large brining bag. Pour in the brine, then add the turkey. Put the bucket in the refrigerator and let it brine for 10 hours. Flip it once halfway through the brining.

4. Take the turkey out of the brine and pat it dry with paper towels. Let it rest for 1 hour.

5. Preheat the smoker to 225°F.

6. Rub the turkey with the butter, getting it under the skin as much as you can. Sprinkle the bird with the salt, pepper, and granulated garlic and set it in a large pan.

7. Smoke the turkey for 8 hours, or until the internal temperature in the thickest part of the thigh reaches 165°F.

8. Let the turkey rest for 15 minutes before carving.

Bacon-Wrapped Smoked and Stuffed Chicken

SERVES 6

PREP TIME:
1 hour
20 minutes

SMOKING TIME:
1 hour
15 minutes

TEMPERATURE:
275°F

WOOD:
Apple

We've established that smoked chicken is delicious. But stuffing boneless chicken breasts with cheese, then wrapping them in bacon and smoking them takes it to another level. This dish comes out amazingly moist and juicy. It's perfect rainy day BBQ.

6 boneless, skinless chicken breasts

¾ cup Poultry Rub (page 164)

3 cups shredded cheddar cheese

12 slices bacon

½ cup store-bought barbecue sauce or Bacon-Flavored BBQ Sauce (page 170)

1. Flatten the chicken breasts with a meat mallet until they are half as thick as when you started.

2. Coat the chicken breasts on both sides with the rub. Set them on a sheet of wax or parchment paper so that there are no spaces between them and they form a large rectangle. Over each chicken breast, evenly spread ½ cup cheddar. Very carefully, roll the entire chicken rectangle into a tight log enclosed in the wax paper. Twist the ends of the wax paper to close and refrigerate the chicken log for 1 hour.

3. Preheat the smoker to 275°F.

4. On another sheet of wax paper, lay out the bacon slices so that there are no spaces between them. Unwrap the chicken log and set it on the edge of the bacon. Carefully roll the chicken on the bacon to make a bacon-wrapped chicken log. Leave the log on the wax paper.

5. Brush the bacon-wrapped log with the barbecue sauce.

6. Cut the wax paper to make two "handles" on each end for lifting the log and placing it in the smoker.

7. Set the chicken in the smoker and carefully remove the wax paper. Smoke for 1 hour 15 minutes, or until the internal temperature reaches 165°F.

8. Slice the log and serve warm.

SMOKING TIP: For a lighter smoky taste, use alder wood. If you have a pellet smoker, set the temperature to 350°F and smoke for 45 minutes, or until the internal temperature reaches 165°F.

PAIR IT WITH: This dish goes well with a glass of pinot noir or chardonnay. Try Smoked Corn Salsa (page 134) on the side.

Smoked Chicken Caesar Salad

SERVES 4

PREP TIME:
15 minutes

SMOKING TIME:
1 hour
30 minutes

TEMPERATURE:
250°F
and 425°F

WOOD:
Alder or apple

Smoked salad, you say? What trickery is this? If you've never charred lettuce before, prepare to have your taste buds blown away. This is a meal that uses the grill on a pellet smoker to char the lettuce. Something magical happens when you do that, but I won't spoil it for you—try this recipe to find out for yourself.

4 boneless, skinless chicken breasts, cut into ½-inch-wide strips

6 tablespoons olive oil, divided

2 teaspoons salt, divided

2 teaspoons freshly ground black pepper, divided

2 teaspoons granulated garlic, divided

6 slices bacon

2 heads romaine lettuce

½ cup grated Romano cheese

1 loaf Italian bread

Butter, at room temperature

1 cup Caesar salad dressing

1. Preheat a pellet smoker to 250°F.

2. Rub the chicken with 2 tablespoons olive oil and then with 1 teaspoon each salt, pepper, and granulated garlic.

3. Smoke the chicken breasts for 1 hour 30 minutes, or until the internal temperature reaches 165°F.

4. At the same time, arrange the bacon on a cooling rack or grill screen (or directly on the smoker grate, perpendicular to the grate). Smoke for about 1 hour 30 minutes, or until the bacon is crisp and browned. Chop the bacon coarsely and set aside.

5. Increase the smoker temperature to 425°F.

6. Halve the heads of lettuce lengthwise. Lay them on a cutting board cut-side up. Drizzle with the remaining 4 tablespoons olive oil. Sprinkle the Romano over the lettuce and then the remaining 1 teaspoon each salt, pepper, and garlic.

7. Place the lettuce cut-side down onto the grill grate. Cook for about 90 seconds. Lettuce cooks very fast, so don't walk away.

8. Remove the lettuce from the grill and place it cut-side up on 4 serving plates.

9. Halve the loaf of bread horizontally, butter both halves, then cut each half into 4 pieces (for a total of 8 pieces). Place the bread on the grill, butter-side down, and toast them.

10. To serve, place the strips of smoked chicken breast over the lettuce. Add the chopped bacon, then drizzle the Caesar dressing over the top. Serve with the toasted bread.

SMOKING TIP: If you want the bacon to stand out, use more and smoke with hickory wood.

PAIR IT WITH: Serve this meal with a sauvignon blanc or pinot gris.

Hunter's Smoked Duck

SERVES 3

PREP TIME:
8 hours
30 minutes

SMOKING TIME:
3 hours

TEMPERATURE:
275°F
and 500°F

WOOD:
Pecan or oak

In Canada, the prairies of Saskatchewan and the Quill Lake region are legendary for duck hunting. I'm not a hunter, but I sure do appreciate a good duck dish. This recipe came from some hunter friends who invited me over to try some. It's not that complicated and it's very good.

8 cups water, divided

½ cup coarse salt

½ cup maple syrup, divided

½ cup pickling spices

1 (4½-pound) whole duck

½ cup orange juice

1. In a saucepan, heat 2 cups water over medium heat. Add the salt, ¼ cup maple syrup, and the pickling spices. Stir until the salt is dissolved.

2. Transfer to a large pot and add the remaining 6 cups water. Cool the brine completely.

3. Trim the duck by removing most of fat inside the body cavity and around the neck. Pierce the skin all over with a needle to help the fat escape while smoking. Avoid sticking the meat with the needle.

4. Put the duck in the brine and refrigerate for 8 hours.

5. Take the duck out of the brine and dry it completely with paper towels.

6. Preheat the smoker to 275°F.

7. Set the duck in the smoker, breast-side up. Make sure the drip pan is in place and directly under the duck. Smoke for 3 hours, or until the internal temperature at the breast reaches 165°F.

8. In a small bowl, mix the orange juice and remaining ¼ cup maple syrup. Take the duck out of the smoker and brush it with the glaze.

9. For crispy skin, increase the temperature of the pellet smoker to 500°F (if you don't have a pellet smoker, do this in the oven). Place the duck in the smoker and check after 5 minutes; don't cook the duck at this temperature for more than 10 minutes.

10. Serve warm.

KNOW YOUR INGREDIENTS: You can swap out the maple syrup for molasses mixed with 1 tablespoon of brown sugar.

PAIR IT WITH: Serve the duck with Smoked Potatoes and Onions (page 125) and pair the meal with a riesling or pinot gris.

Applewood-Smoked Chicken

SERVES 4

PREP TIME:
20 minutes

SMOKING TIME:
1 hour
30 minutes

TEMPERATURE:
275°F

WOOD:
Apple

Hot or cold, smoked chicken is a great go-to dish for dinner or lunch! It's less time-consuming to smoke than pork or beef, and if you're planning a picnic, smoked chicken makes for an amazing sandwich. In this recipe, I truss the chicken and smoke it whole, but feel free to spatchcock it instead, following the instructions on page 19 for spatchcocking a turkey.

1 (5- to 6-pound) whole chicken

½ lemon

1 tablespoon olive oil

7 cups Poultry Rub (page 164)

4 or 5 rosemary sprigs

1. Pat the chicken dry with paper towels. Rub the chicken with the lemon half, then drizzle the olive oil over it. Generously sprinkle the rub all over the inside and outside of the chicken. Rub it into the skin.

2. Put the rosemary sprigs inside the chicken. Truss the chicken by crossing the drumsticks and tying them together with kitchen twine. Then, tie the wings close to the body with another length of twine.

3. Preheat the smoker to 275°F.

4. Place the chicken breast-side down in the smoker and cover it with aluminum foil. Smoke for 30 minutes.

5. Turn the chicken breast-side up, then smoke, covered, for 1 hour, or until the internal temperature in the thickest part of the thigh reaches 165°F.

6. Wrap the cooked chicken in butcher paper or aluminum foil and let rest for 10 minutes. Cut the twine and serve.

PAIR IT WITH: I love to serve this with sides like Smoked Potato Salad with Bacon (page 126) and garlic bread. If you like wine, try a chilled malbec or Bordeaux.

Smoked Cornish Hens

SERVES 4

PREP TIME:
1 hour

SMOKING TIME:
2 hours
30 minutes

TEMPERATURE:
250°F

WOOD:
Hickory and/
or cherry

This is a fun dish to smoke because everyone feels like royalty when they have their own hen. If you're serving more than four people, split the hens down the middle. Whether it's a picnic or part of a big dinner, these delicious and delicately smoked Cornish hens never disappoint. Especially if served with a paper crown.

4 Cornish hens

¼ cup olive oil

½ cup Poultry Rub (page 164)

2 lemons, cut into quarters

4 rosemary sprigs

1. Pat the hens dry with paper towels and let them come to room temperature, 45 minutes to 1 hour.

2. Preheat the smoker to 250°F.

3. In a small bowl, mix the olive oil with the poultry rub. Rub the inside and outside of the birds with this mixture.

4. Put 2 lemon quarters and a sprig of rosemary inside each bird. Tie the legs together with kitchen twine.

5. Smoke the hens for 2 hours 30 minutes, or until the internal temperature reaches 165°F.

6. Remove the hens, place on two large cutting boards, and let rest for at least 15 minutes.

7. Remove the twine, lemons, and rosemary and serve.

PAIR IT WITH: Serve with Smoked Vegetable Casserole (page 129) and pair it with a sauvignon blanc or chardonnay or even a zinfandel rosé.

SMOKING TIP: If you want to stuff the hens, with corn bread for instance, increase the smoker temperature to 275°F and smoke the birds until the internal temp reaches 160°F.

Sichuan-Inspired Tea-Smoked Duck

SERVES 4

PREP TIME:
7 hours

SMOKING TIME:
2 hours
30 minutes

TEMPERATURE:
275°F

WOOD:
Cherry
or maple

I first tried this in a restaurant in Toronto's Chinatown. The chef there worked in Hong Kong a long time ago, so he had adapted the duck to British tastes. Duck breasts are easy to smoke. With this special brine and tea smoke, you'll discover a new taste experience.

4 cups water

⅓ cup coarse salt

⅓ cup packed light brown sugar

1 teaspoon coarsely
  ground black pepper

4 tablespoons black tea
  leaves, divided

2 cups ice

2 pounds boneless,
  skin-on duck breasts

3 tablespoons sesame oil

1. In a large pot, bring the water to a boil. Add the salt and brown sugar and let dissolve. Add the pepper and 2 tablespoons tea, then remove it from the heat. Add the ice and place the brine in the refrigerator until it's cold, about 45 minutes.

2. Place the duck breasts in a 1-gallon zip-top bag. Pour in the cooled brine. Seal the bag, pressing out all the air. Put the bag back in the pot and refrigerate for 5 hours.

3. Remove the duck from the bag and pat it dry with paper towels. Put it on a plate and refrigerate, uncovered, for 1 hour.

4. Preheat the smoker to 275°F.

5. Rub the duck with the sesame oil and place it in the smoker. Place the remaining 2 tablespoons tea in a small metal dish in a rack below the duck (when the tea stops smoking, remove the container).

6. Smoke the duck for 2 hours 30 minutes, or until the internal temperature reaches 165°F.

7. Serve warm.

Smoked Tex-Mex Chicken Tacos

SERVES 4

PREP TIME:
30 minutes

SMOKING TIME:
3 hours

TEMPERATURE:
250°F
and 425°F

WOOD:
Apple
or cherry

Taco bars are always a hit at gatherings and they give people something to do. Who doesn't love to build their own taco from an assortment of fun toppings? With this recipe, it's easy to set up a Tex-Mex meal for lunch or a casual dinner.

¼ cup olive oil

½ cup Poultry Rub (page 164)

2 tablespoons minced garlic

1 teaspoon cayenne pepper (optional)

1 (4-pound) whole chicken

2 limes, cut into wedges

1½ cups salsa

1 cup sour cream

1 cup guacamole

12 (8-inch) flour tortillas

1. In a small bowl, mix together the oil, poultry rub, garlic, and cayenne (if using).

2. Rub the whole outside of the chicken with the seasoning mixture. Tie the legs together with kitchen twine and tuck the wings behind. To do this, hold one of the wings in your hand. Then, lift that side of the bird up a couple of inches and tuck the wing underneath the back. Then, lower the bird. Do the same thing for the other side.

3. Preheat the smoker to 250°F.

4. Smoke the chicken for 3 hours, or until the internal temperature at the thighs reaches 165°F. If you want the skin crispy and you have a pellet smoker, increase the temperature to 425°F when the internal temperature at the breast is 150°F.

5. Remove the chicken from the smoker and let rest for at least 15 minutes.

6. Carve up the chicken breast and the thighs into slices and set the pieces on a serving tray.

7. Serve with the limes, salsa, sour cream, and guacamole in separate bowls, next to a stack of warm tortillas.

Smoked Javanese-Style Chicken Satay with Spicy Peanut Sauce

SERVES 4

PREP TIME:
1 hour
30 minutes

SMOKE TIME:
1 hour
30 minutes

TEMPERATURE:
275°F

WOOD:
Cherry
or hickory

Want to try something different on the smoker? More than just chicken kebabs, this recipe brings uniquely complex flavors to your meal. It's my take on a traditional recipe that originated on the island of Java in Indonesia. Satay started out (and still is) a "street food." This dish is found all over Southeast Asia, and everyone's recipe is a little different.

⅓ cup well-shaken canned light coconut milk

¼ cup sesame oil

2 tablespoons fresh lime juice, divided

1 tablespoon grated peeled fresh ginger

3 garlic cloves, minced

1½ teaspoons smoked paprika

1 teaspoon ground turmeric

1 teaspoon salt

1 teaspoon freshly ground black pepper

2 pounds boneless, skinless chicken breasts, cut into 1½-inch cubes

2 cups Spicy Peanut Sauce (page 174), divided

2 tablespoons chopped fresh cilantro

1. In a medium bowl, whisk together the coconut milk, sesame oil, 1 tablespoon lime juice, the ginger, garlic, smoked paprika, turmeric, salt, and pepper. Add the chicken to the marinade and coat it completely. Cover and chill for 1 hour.

2. Take the chicken out and let it reach room temperature before smoking, about 30 minutes.

3. Preheat the smoker to 275°F. If you are using wooden skewers, soak them in water for at least 30 minutes.

4. Thread the skewers through the chicken cubes, leaving about 1 inch of space on each end.

5. Smoke the skewers for 30 minutes, then rotate. Smoke for another 30 minutes.

6. Remove the chicken and coat with 1 cup peanut sauce. Smoke for another 30 minutes, or until the internal temperature reaches 165°F.

7. Sprinkle the chopped cilantro over the chicken and serve with the remaining 1 cup peanut sauce.

MAKE IT EASIER: You can substitute 2 tablespoons of Thai red curry paste for the pepper, paprika, turmeric, and ginger.

Rum-Brined and Smoked Turkey Legs

SERVES 6

PREP TIME:
11 hours

SMOKING TIME:
2 hours
30 minutes

TEMPERATURE:
275°F

WOOD:
Cherry/
hickory mix
or apple

You probably know this fun food from Renaissance fairs and theme parks, but turkey legs are also entertaining out in the backyard. The smoker makes this meal super easy, while the brine keeps the turkey moist with a hint of sweetness that lets the smoky taste go deep. The turkey needs to be brined overnight, so plan accordingly.

10 cups water, divided

¼ cup coarse salt

½ cup maple syrup or ¼ cup light brown sugar

1 cup dark rum

4 bay leaves

1 tablespoon mixed peppercorns

6 turkey drumsticks

¾ cup plus 2 tablespoons Poultry Rub (page 164)

1. In a large pot, bring 2 cups water to almost boiling. Add the salt and maple syrup and stir until the salt has dissolved. Remove from the heat and stir in the rum, bay leaves, peppercorns, and remaining 8 cups water. Set aside to cool.

2. When the brine has cooled, add the turkey. Store in the refrigerator for 10 hours or overnight.

3. Preheat the smoker to 275°F.

4. Take the turkey legs out of the brine and quickly rinse them under cold water. Then pat them well with paper towels. Season the turkey with the poultry rub.

5. Smoke the turkey for about 2 hours 30 minutes, or until the internal temperature in the thickest part of the leg reaches 165°F.

6. Let the turkey rest for at least 10 minutes before serving.

KNOW YOUR INGREDIENTS: Try molasses instead of maple syrup for a darker color and not-as-sweet finish.

Beer-Brined Smoked Chicken Legs

SERVES 4

PREP TIME:
3 hours

SMOKING TIME:
2 hours to
2 hours
30 minutes

TEMPERATURE:
275°F

WOOD:
Apple
or pecan

For an informal lunch or dinner with some friends or the family, these smoked chicken drumsticks are easy to make. With the beer-brining and spices, they're going to be moist and the flavor will soak into the meat. Take them for a picnic and eat them cold.

8 chicken drumsticks

1½ cups cold water

2 (12-ounce) bottles beer or ale

½ cup coarse salt

½ cup packed light brown sugar

1 tablespoon minced garlic

1 tablespoon Dijon mustard

2 teaspoons chopped fresh rosemary

3 tablespoons olive oil

¼ cup Poultry Rub (page 164)

1. Place the drumsticks in a large container that has a lid.

2. Fill a 1-gallon or larger pitcher with the water and beer. Stir in the salt and continue to stir until it's completely dissolved. Then stir in the brown sugar, making sure it's also dissolved. Mix in the garlic, mustard, and rosemary.

3. Pour the brine over the drumsticks, cover the container, and refrigerate for 2 hours 30 minutes.

4. Preheat the smoker to 275°F.

5. Rinse the drumsticks to get rid of the excess salt. Then pat them dry with paper towels. Brush them with the olive oil and rub with the poultry rub until they're coated all over.

6. Place the drumsticks in the smoker. Make sure the drip pan is in place under them. Smoke for 2 hours to 2 hours 30 minutes, or until the internal temperature reaches 165°F.

7. Serve warm.

KNOW YOUR INGREDIENTS: For more spice, add 2 tablespoons of red pepper flakes to the brine and ½ teaspoon of cayenne pepper to the rub.

Jerked Chicken

SERVES 4

PREP TIME:
5 hours

SMOKING TIME:
2 hours

TEMPERATURE:
275°F

WOOD:
Hickory

It is thought that the term "jerk" or "jerky" comes from an old Spanish word *charqui*, which was a word for smoked, dried meat. The spiciness of this marinade stands up well to a strong smoke. Do yourself a favor and get your butcher to spatchcock the chicken. Or do it yourself, following the instructions on page 19 for spatchcocking a turkey.

½ cup fresh lime juice

½ cup soy sauce

¼ cup olive oil

2 tablespoons dark rum

2 tablespoons molasses

¼ cup packed light brown sugar

½ cup minced onions

3 tablespoons minced garlic

2 habanero peppers, seeded and minced

¼ cup Poultry Rub (page 164)

2 tablespoons ground allspice

1 tablespoon ground ginger

1 (4-pound) whole chicken, spatchcocked

1. In a medium bowl, whisk together the lime juice, soy sauce, olive oil, rum, molasses, brown sugar, onions, garlic, habaneros, poultry rub, allspice, and ground ginger.

2. Set the chicken in a large, deep dish and pour the marinade over it. Refrigerate the chicken, covered, for 5 hours. Flip after 2 hours 30 minutes.

3. Preheat the smoker to 275°F.

4. Put the chicken skin-side up in the middle of the smoker. Smoke the chicken for about 2 hours, or until the internal temperature reaches 165°F.

5. Remove the chicken from the smoker and let rest at room temperature for 15 minutes before serving.

PAIR IT WITH: For side dishes, serve Smoked Cherry Tomatoes (page 142) and Smoked Corn on the Cob (page 133). A nice cold lager beer goes well with this spicy chicken.

Bourbon Smoked Chicken

SERVES 4

PREP TIME:
6 hours

SMOKING TIME:
3 hours
45 minutes

TEMPERATURE:
225°F

WOOD:
Apple
or cherry

Bourbon in both the brine and the BBQ sauce adds a Southern touch to this delightfully moist, smoked chicken. Because I used a BBQ sauce, I didn't need to rub in seasoning after brining.

16 cups water, divided

1 cup coarse salt

⅓ cup Poultry Rub (page 164)

Grated zest of 1 lemon

2 tablespoons minced garlic

1 tablespoon mixed peppercorns

1 tablespoon chopped fresh rosemary

8 tablespoons bourbon, divided

4 cups ice

1 (4-pound) whole chicken

2½ cups Bacon-Flavored BBQ Sauce (page 170), divided

1. In a large pot, heat 2 cups water until almost boiling. Add the salt and stir to dissolve. Remove from the heat. Stir in the poultry rub, lemon zest, garlic, peppercorns, and rosemary. Add the remaining 14 cups water. Then add 6 tablespoons bourbon and the ice and let the brine cool completely.

2. Place the chicken in the brine, cover the pot, and refrigerate for 5 hours.

3. Preheat the smoker to 225°F.

4. Rinse the brine off the chicken and pat dry with paper towels.

5. Smoke the chicken for 3 hours 15 minutes.

6. Remove the chicken and brush it with ½ cup barbecue sauce. Smoke for another 30 minutes, or until the internal temperature reaches 165°F.

7. Remove the chicken and let rest for 15 minutes.

8. Mix the remaining 2 tablespoons bourbon into the remaining 2 cups barbecue sauce and serve it alongside the smoked chicken.

Herb-Brined Smoked Chicken

SERVES 4

PREP TIME:
5 hours

SMOKING TIME:
3 hours

TEMPERATURE:
275°F

WOOD:
Hickory
or pecan

There are so many ways to get great flavors from smoked poultry. With this brine, the chicken will be moist, tender, and full of rich herbal and vegetable flavors. It can stand up to a strong or sweet smoke.

3 cups water

⅓ cup coarse salt

⅓ cup packed light brown sugar

1 small onion, halved

1 celery stalk with leaves

2 tablespoons minced garlic

2 teaspoons grated lemon zest

1 tablespoon chopped fresh parsley

1 tablespoon chopped fresh oregano

2 thyme sprigs

1 rosemary sprig

1 bay leaf

3 cups ice

1 (4-pound) whole chicken

2 tablespoons olive oil

3 tablespoons Poultry Rub (page 164)

5 fresh sage leaves

1. In a large pot, heat the water to almost boiling. Add the salt, stirring until it's dissolved. Add the brown sugar and stir to dissolve. Add the onion, celery, garlic, lemon zest, parsley, oregano, thyme, rosemary, and bay leaf. Remove the pot from the heat.

2. Add the ice to the brine. Cover the pot and put it in the refrigerator for about 45 minutes.

3. When the brine is cold, put the chicken in a 1-gallon zip-top bag. Discard the onion and celery from the brine and pour the brine over the chicken. Seal the bag and refrigerate for 4 hours, turning it once each hour.

4. Preheat the smoker to 275°F.

5. Take the chicken out of the brine. Use paper towels to dry the chicken inside and out. Rub the olive oil all over the skin, then rub with the poultry rub. Place the sage leaves inside the bird.

6. Smoke the chicken for 3 hours, or until the internal temperature reaches 165°F.

7. Let it rest for 10 minutes, then serve.

KNOW YOUR INGREDIENTS: Try a combination of ¼ cup of brown sugar and ¼ cup of molasses instead of just brown sugar.

Smoked Chicken Thighs with Wasabi-Soy Marinade

SERVES 4

PREP TIME:
5 hours

SMOKING TIME:
1 hour

TEMPERATURE:
275°F

WOOD:
Maple
or pecan

Wasabi is usually associated with sushi and seafood, but it's wonderful with poultry, too. When you add it to a marinade with soy sauce, ginger, and sesame, you'll get an excellent savory dish with a nice kick of spice, inspired by some of the signature flavors of Japan.

¼ cup soy sauce, plus
   more for serving

2 tablespoons rice vinegar

1 tablespoon grated
   peeled fresh ginger

2 teaspoons wasabi paste,
   plus more for serving

2 teaspoons chili-garlic sauce

1 tablespoon sesame seeds

1 tablespoon minced garlic

3 tablespoons sesame
   oil, divided

2 pounds bone-in, skin-on
   chicken thighs

1. In a container with a cover, mix together the soy sauce, vinegar, ginger, wasabi, chili-garlic sauce, sesame seeds, garlic, and 1 tablespoon sesame oil.

2. Add the chicken thighs and coat them completely. Cover the container and refrigerate for 4 hours.

3. Remove the chicken thighs from the marinade and pat them dry with paper towels. Let them rest for another 45 minutes to 1 hour at room temperature.

4. Preheat the smoker to 275°F.

5. Brush the chicken with the remaining 2 tablespoons sesame oil.

6. Place the chicken thighs in the smoker and smoke for 1 hour, or until the internal temperature reaches 165°F.

7. Serve warm, with some soy sauce and wasabi on the side for dipping.

KNOW YOUR INGREDIENTS: If you can't get wasabi, use red pepper flakes. Try cider vinegar instead of the rice vinegar and add 1 tablespoon of maple syrup to the marinade. It'll be a little sweeter and it's a nice way to offset the wasabi.

3-2-1 Smoked Ribs,
page 46

Chapter 3

Pork

THERE IS SO MUCH THAT you can do with pork on the smoker. You have ribs, chops, tenderloin, shoulder, sausage, and, of course, BACON, including pork belly. Low-and-slow smoking makes for fall-off-the-bone-tender pork. Smoked pork also develops a beautiful "bark" that I'll show you how to make. This chapter covers flavors from Argentina, Mexico, the Caribbean, and Spain. You'll also get to choose from a wide variety of dishes that come from different corners of the United States. With pork, you can use stronger flavored woods for smoking than you can with poultry. In general, the lighter woods get overwhelmed by the spice and marinades. And as always, feel free to experiment with different ingredients in your wet and dry brines!

Bacon, Pastrami, and Smoked Pork Cheeseburgers

SERVES 4

PREP TIME:
15 minutes

SMOKING TIME:
1 hour

TEMPERATURE:
275°F

WOOD:
Hickory
or oak

We had bacon left over from a show and decided to try an over-the-top experiment with it and . . . it worked! This super burger is as impressive to make as it is delicious to serve. Fair warning: It's not for the faint-hearted.

2 pounds ground pork

¼ cup jarred garlic puree

Salt

Freshly ground black pepper

Granulated garlic

4 slices smoked bacon

1 pound pastrami, sliced

12 arugula leaves

4 large hamburger buns,
split and toasted

4 slices beefsteak tomato

4 slices cheese, such as
provolone, cheddar,
American, or Swiss

Favorite burger sauce,
for serving

1. Preheat the smoker to 275°F.

2. In a bowl, mix together the ground pork and garlic puree.

3. Divide the burger mixture into 4 equal portions (about 8 ounces each) and shape them into balls. Then flatten them out a bit into patties. Use a soup spoon to make a dent in the center of each patty to help it cook more evenly and keep its shape.

4. Sprinkle both sides of the patties with a generous amount of salt, pepper, and granulated garlic to taste.

5. Smoke the burgers for 40 minutes.

6. Arrange the bacon and pastrami on two different cooking racks and set in the smoker. Continue to smoke the burgers, bacon, and pastrami for another 20 minutes, or until the internal temperature of the burgers reaches 160°F.

7. To assemble, place 3 arugula leaves on the bottom of each bun. Add a slice of tomato, a burger, a slice of cheese, some pastrami, and a slice of bacon to each burger. Squirt your favorite sauce over the burgers, add the top bun, and serve.

MAKE IT EASIER: If you can get smoked pork belly, which has already been cooked, you can heat it up and substitute that for the bacon.

3-2-1 Smoked Ribs

SERVES 6

PREP TIME:
20 minutes

SMOKING TIME:
6 hours

TEMPERATURE:
225°F

WOOD:
Mesquite

What could be more laid-back than fall-off-the-bone ribs? It's as easy as 3 hours unwrapped, 2 hours wrapped, and 1 hour unwrapped. This recipe may have originated in St. Louis, but now it has spread beyond the BBQ Belt and belongs to everyone. To make this recipe, you'll need a full 15 feet of butcher paper.

3 racks St. Louis-style pork ribs

1 to 2 cups Pork Rub (page 165)

1 cup apple juice

3 cups Bacon-Flavored BBQ sauce (optional; page 170)

1. Preheat the smoker to 225°F.

2. Remove and discard the membrane from the bone side of the ribs. Cover both sides of the ribs with the pork rub.

3. Smoke the ribs for 3 hours. Fill a spray bottle with the apple juice.

4. Take the ribs out and place them on a board. (Those ribs will be hot, so handle them with BBQ mitts.) Using a spray bottle, give them a squirt or two of the apple juice on both sides.

5. Tightly wrap each rack of ribs with the butcher paper.

6. Place the wrapped ribs in the smoker and smoke for 2 hours.

7. Then take them out and unwrap them. If desired, spread the sauce all over some (or all) of the ribs.

8. Return them to the smoker and smoke for 1 hour. If some of the ribs are sauced, place them below the unsauced ribs.

9. Carefully take the ribs out of the smoker and let them rest for 15 minutes before serving.

PAIR IT WITH: Enjoy these ribs with your favorite side dishes, like Smoked Mac 'n' Cheese (page 120) or Smoked Corn on the Cob (page 133).

Pulled Pork Sandwiches

SERVES 6

PREP TIME:
15 minutes

SMOKING TIME:
6 to 9 hours

TEMPERATURE:
225°F

WOOD:
Mesquite
or hickory

I wake up thinking about pulled pork sandwiches. In fact, a pulled pork sandwich is my wife's idea of a romantic dinner. Lucky me! These originated in the American South, but now they are enjoyed everywhere. At 225°F, the pork should take about 1 hour 30 minutes per pound to cook.

1 cup Pork Rub (page 165)

¼ cup packed light brown sugar

4 to 6 pounds boneless
  Boston butt

1 cup Dijon mustard
  (or your favorite)

1 cup apple juice

6 kaiser rolls, split and toasted

Favorite sauce, for serving

1. Preheat the smoker to 225°F.

2. In a small bowl, mix together the pork rub and brown sugar. Slather the meat with the mustard, then generously sprinkle the pork rub mixture over the meat, rubbing it all over.

3. Smoke the pork for 4 hours. Fill a spray bottle with apple juice.

4. Remove the pork, spray with the apple juice, and wrap tightly in butcher paper. Smoke it for another 2 hours, or until the internal temperature reaches 195°F.

5. Let the pork rest for 1 hour, then shred it.

6. Serve on toasted kaiser rolls with your favorite sauce.

PAIR IT WITH: Pulled pork is marvelous when you spoon some Smoked Mac 'n' Cheese (page 120) on it.

KNOW YOUR INGREDIENTS: Boston butt is a cut of pork that comes from the upper part of the pig's shoulder from the front leg. Sometimes it is sold with the bone in, but I prefer the boneless butt.

Argentine-Style Smoked Boston Butt

SERVES 4

PREP TIME:
30 minutes

SMOKING TIME:
6 hours

TEMPERATURE:
250°F

WOOD:
Oak

This recipe was inspired by a genuine Argentine pitmaster named Federico. He uses an injector to add the moisture to the meat that you would usually get by brining it. It's not an exact substitute for brining, but it sure is a great alternative. This recipe uses an injector, too, so if you want to give it a go, look for them at Walmart or on Amazon.

4 to 6 pounds boneless Boston butt

1 cup defatted chicken stock

3 tablespoons light brown sugar, divided

1 teaspoon Worcestershire sauce

¼ cup Pork Rub (page 165)

1 tablespoon chipotle powder

1 teaspoon cayenne pepper

1 cup apple juice

1. Preheat the smoker to 250°F and fill the water pan.

2. If the pork has a fat cap (layer of fat), separate it from the meat with a sharp knife. Set aside.

3. In a measuring cup, mix together the chicken stock, 1 tablespoon brown sugar, and the Worcestershire sauce. Pull it into the meat injector and inject it into the pork all over.

4. In a small bowl, mix together the pork rub, chipotle powder, and cayenne. Rub it all over the meat.

5. Replace the fat cap on the side of the meat it came from and tie it in place with butcher's twine.

6. Smoke the pork butt for 3 hours. Fill a spray bottle with the apple juice.

7. Spray with the apple juice and tightly wrap the pork with aluminum foil. It's a good idea to place wrapped meat on a small baking dish so it doesn't get punctured.

8. Return the meat to the smoker and smoke for another 3 hours, or until the internal temperature reaches 205°F.

9. Unwrap the pork and let it rest for 15 minutes before cutting into it.

MAKE IT EASIER: Save some time and don't remove the fat. Just make crisscrosses on it with a sharp knife and then rub in the seasoning.

Smoked Pork Souvlaki

SERVES 6

PREP TIME:
1 hour
30 minutes

SMOKING TIME:
2 hours
30 minutes

TEMPERATURE:
275°F

WOOD:
Oak

The Greeks have been cooking meat on skewers since the Bronze Age. Souvlaki is a classic fast food in Greece, usually served with pita bread, fried potatoes, lemon wedges, and sauces. Yum! I love how these marinated smoked pork cubes with a classic tzatziki sauce on the side take you to the Mediterranean without leaving your backyard. *Yamas!*

FOR THE SOUVLAKI

3 to 4 pounds boneless pork loin, cut into 1-inch cubes

½ cup olive oil

Juice of 2 lemons

3 tablespoons distilled white vinegar

2 tablespoons dried oregano

2 teaspoons honey

1 teaspoon salt

1 teaspoon freshly ground black pepper

FOR SERVING

Extra-virgin olive oil, for brushing and drizzling

6 pita breads

Salt

Dried oregano

2 red onions, sliced

1 lemon, cut into wedges

2½ cups Smoked Garlic Tzatziki Sauce (page 122)

TO MAKE THE SOUVLAKI

1. In a large bowl, toss the pork cubes, olive oil, lemon juice, vinegar, oregano, honey, salt, and pepper. Make sure all the pork is coated in the marinade, then cover with plastic wrap and refrigerate for 1 hour, mixing halfway through.

2. Preheat the smoker to 275°F. Meanwhile, if using wooden skewers, soak them in water for at least 30 minutes.

3. Thread the pieces of pork onto the skewers. Do not squish the pieces together, but do not leave space between the pieces either.

4. Smoke the pork skewers for 2 hours 30 minutes, or until the internal temperature reaches 155°F.

FOR SERVING

5. While the pork is smoking, brush some olive oil on both sides of the pitas. Season with salt and oregano. When the souvlaki is done, pop the pitas in the smoker for 3 minutes.

6. To serve, spread the red onion slices on a serving platter. Then place the pork skewers on top of the onions and drizzle with some extra-virgin olive oil and a good squeeze of lemon juice. Serve with the warmed pitas and tzatziki sauce on the side.

SMOKING TIP: If you have a pellet smoker, crank the heat to 375°F for the last 5 minutes to get the meat more caramelized.

Smoked Italian Sausage with Peppers and Onions

SERVES 6

PREP TIME:
1 hour

SMOKING TIME:
3 hours

TEMPERATURE:
250°F

WOOD:
Maple or oak

I have a friend who owns a restaurant in Toronto, but who was originally from Buenos Aires. He told me that the Italian influence on cooking in that city was substantial. This dish is typically called *choripán*, which is just bread and sausage. It's the chimichurri that makes it Argentine.

3 pounds hot or sweet Italian sausage links

½ cup whole-grain mustard

2 tablespoons chopped fresh cilantro

1 cup chimichurri, store-bought or homemade (page 171)

1 teaspoon freshly ground black pepper

2 large yellow or red onions

2 large red or green bell peppers

1. Pat the sausages dry with paper towels and set them uncovered in the refrigerator for 1 hour to let them dry some more.

2. Preheat the smoker to 250°F.

3. Place the sausages in the smoker. Make sure there is space between the links to let the smoke flow freely around them. Smoke for 3 hours, or until the internal temperature reaches 165°F.

4. Meanwhile, in a bowl, mix together the mustard, cilantro, chimichurri, and pepper. Cover and refrigerate until serving.

5. About 15 minutes before the sausages are done, cut the onions into ½-inch slices. Cut the top off the peppers, remove the seeds, and cut into rings and then half-rings.

6. On the stovetop in a skillet over medium heat, fry the onions and peppers until browned and slightly charred, about 5 minutes. (Or if you have a pellet smoker, increase the temperature to 425°F and cook them on the grill.) When they're done, place them on a serving board or a large platter.

7. To serve, set the sausages next to the onions and peppers and brush everything with the reserved mustard/chimichurri sauce.

KNOW YOUR INGREDIENTS: If you like spicier food, when the sausages are done, drizzle them with your favorite hot sauce or use 1 teaspoon of red pepper flakes instead of black pepper.

Smoked Pork Loin

SERVES 4

PREP TIME:
20 minutes

SMOKING TIME:
2 hours
30 minutes

TEMPERATURE:
275°F

WOOD:
Maple, pecan,
or peach

Some pitmasters call pork loin a "blank slate" because you can impart so many different flavors to it. When I don't have all day to smoke, this simple smoked pork loin is the recipe to make. It's great for sandwiches, so you might want to make it in the morning for a picnic lunch. At this temperature, the pork cooks for about 30 minutes per pound.

5 pounds pork loin

¼ cup olive oil

½ cup Pork Rub (page 165)

1 tablespoon light brown sugar

1. Preheat the smoker to 275°F.

2. With a sharp knife, crisscross the layer of fat on the pork loin. Then brush the pork with the olive oil.

3. In a small bowl, mix the pork rub and brown sugar together. Rub it all over and into the pork loin.

4. Smoke the pork for 2 hours 30 minutes, or until the internal temperature reaches 145°F. Do not overcook it!

5. Remove the pork from the smoker and let rest for at least 15 minutes. Serve warm.

KNOW YOUR INGREDIENTS: If you want to give your pork a little more flavor, brush it with my Bacon-Flavored BBQ Sauce (page 170). If you want to give it a little more spice, add 2 teaspoons of cayenne pepper to the rub.

Smoked Pork Chops

SERVES 4

PREP TIME:
10 minutes

SMOKING TIME:
1 hour
15 minutes

TEMPERATURE:
225°F

WOOD:
Hickory or
mesquite

Low and slow may be the usual way to go, but if you want a smoked pork dinner fast, you'll want to try these chops. You can also make these with bone-in pork chops, and it's just as effortless and delicious.

½ cup Pork Rub (page 165)

1 tablespoon light brown sugar

8 boneless center-cut pork loin chops (at least 1 inch thick)

2 tablespoons olive oil

1 tablespoon apple cider vinegar

1 cup apple juice

1. Preheat the smoker to 225°F.

2. In a small bowl, mix the pork rub with the brown sugar. Brush the pork chops with the olive oil and season them on both sides with the pork rub mixtur.

3. Mix the apple juice with the tablespoon of apple cider vinegar in a spray bottle. Place the chops in the smoker and cook them for 1 hour and 15 minutes. Every 30 minutes or so, spritz them with the apple juice mixture. When their internal temperature reaches 145°F, the chops are ready to come out.

SMOKING TIP: Since these chops don't take too long to cook, you can smoke them with mesquite and you'll get a nice color on them.

KNOW YOUR INGREDIENTS: I like my pork chops spicy, so I add 2 teaspoons of cayenne pepper to the rub.

PAIR IT WITH: Serve with Bacon-Flavored BBQ Sauce (page 170) or some Chimichurri Sauce (page 171) drizzled on top.

Smoked Spicy Baby Back Ribs

SERVES 8

PREP TIME:
8 hours

SMOKING TIME:
2 hours

TEMPERATURE:
250°F

WOOD:
Cherry and
hickory mixed

Baby back ribs are good any time of the year, but especially in nice summer weather. That way, you can hang out with your family and friends while you're smoking and basting.

8 pounds baby back ribs

1 cup Pork Rub (page 165), divided

1 teaspoon coarse salt

1 teaspoon ground cumin

1 teaspoon chipotle powder

2 teaspoons cayenne pepper

1 tablespoon red pepper flakes

1 cup apple cider

½ cup apple cider vinegar

1. Remove the membrane from the bone side of the ribs with a small, sharp knife.

2. In a bowl, mix together ¾ cup pork rub, the salt, cumin, chipotle, cayenne, and red pepper flakes. Rub the pork rub mixture all over the ribs. Wrap them tightly in plastic wrap and refrigerate for 8 hours.

3. Preheat the smoker to 250°F.

4. In a bowl, mix together the apple cider, vinegar, and the remaining ¼ cup pork rub.

5. Place the ribs in the smoker bone-side down. Smoke for 2 hours, basting them with the vinegar mixture every 30 minutes, until the internal temperature reaches 145°F.

6. Let the ribs rest for at least 10 minutes before serving.

KNOW YOUR INGREDIENTS: If you want your ribs even spicier, add your favorite hot sauce to the basting mixture. Or you can add a minced habanero, jalapeño, or Scotch bonnet pepper, seeded, to the basting sauce.

Smoked Candied Bacon

SERVES 4

PREP TIME:
10 minutes

SMOKING TIME:
35 minutes

TEMPERATURE:
275°F

WOOD:
Maple
or pecan

This recipe must have been concocted near a county fair because it's so much fun. Some folks call it "pig candy." I think it's great by itself or as a topping on burgers and sandwiches. It's easy to make, too, so you don't have an excuse not to eat it!

12 slices thick-cut bacon

¾ cup packed light brown sugar

3 tablespoons maple syrup

2 teaspoons freshly ground black pepper

1. Preheat the smoker to 275°F.

2. Arrange the bacon slices on a wire rack. Set on the middle rack of the smoker and smoke the bacon for 15 minutes. Flip the slices over and cook for 5 more minutes.

3. Meanwhile, in a small bowl, mix together the brown sugar, maple syrup, and pepper.

4. Take the bacon out of the smoker and brush both sides with the maple syrup mixture. Return the bacon to the smoker and smoke for another 15 minutes, or until the edges are crisp and the center is caramelized. For a deeper flavor, keep basting with the maple syrup mixture every 5 minutes.

SMOKING TIP: If you have a pellet smoker, set it to 400°F and cook the bacon for 25 minutes. At that temperature, you have to repeat basting with the maple syrup mixture every 5 minutes.

Smoked Pork Belly Ends

SERVES 6

PREP TIME:
30 minutes

SMOKING TIME:
3 hours
15 minutes

TEMPERATURE:
275°F

WOOD:
Cherry
or pecan

Just like the flavorful, fatty, burnt ends of brisket, these pork belly ends are more than an appetizer; they're a main attraction. Pork belly, when it's smoked and sliced, is what we call bacon. And everyone knows that everything is better with bacon.

1 cup Pork Rub (page 165)

1 tablespoon cayenne pepper

8 tablespoons light brown sugar, divided

2 pounds pork belly, skin removed

4 tablespoons (1 stick) unsalted butter, cut into pats

1 cup Bacon-Flavored BBQ Sauce (page 170)

1. Preheat the smoker to 275°F.

2. In a small bowl, mix together the pork rub, cayenne, and 2 tablespoons brown sugar. Cut the pork belly into 1½-inch squares and generously sprinkle the seasoning all over them. Arrange them on a wire rack.

3. Smoke the pork belly squares for 2 hours.

4. Remove the pork belly squares and put them on a sheet pan. Sprinkle with the remaining 6 tablespoons brown sugar and dot with the butter.

5. Return to the smoker and smoke for 1 hour.

6. Take the pan out of the smoker, add the BBQ sauce to the pork belly, and stir it all together. Return the pan to the smoker and cook for 15 more minutes.

7. Let the pork belly rest for 5 to 10 minutes before serving.

KNOW YOUR INGREDIENTS: You can substitute chipotle for the cayenne pepper for a smokier taste. Also, try using maple syrup instead of brown sugar for a slightly sweeter finish.

Smoked Pork Leg

SERVES 10

PREP TIME:
9 hours

SMOKING TIME:
10 to 12 hours

TEMPERATURE:
275°F

WOOD:
Hickory
or oak

This is a recipe for celebrations! Whether it's for sandwiches or as the main course of a sit-down holiday dinner, it's worth the wait.

1 cup Pork Rub (page 165)

½ cup packed light brown sugar

2 tablespoons coarse salt

1 tablespoon dried thyme

1 tablespoon ground cumin

2 teaspoons cayenne pepper

1 (12- to 14-pound) bone-in leg of pork

1 cup apple juice

1 tablespoon fresh lime juice

1. In a medium bowl, mix together the pork rub, brown sugar, salt, thyme, cumin, and cayenne. Rub generous amounts of the mixture onto the leg of pork. Wrap it in plastic wrap and refrigerate for 8 hours.

2. Take it out of the fridge and let it come to room temperature, about 1 hour.

3. Preheat the smoker to 275°F.

4. Smoke the pork leg for 4 hours, or until the internal temperature reaches 145°F.

5. Mix the apple and lime juice in a spray bottle. Take the pork leg out of the smoker, spray it with the juice, then set it on a sheet of aluminum foil. Pour the rest of the juice on the meat, then wrap it up in the foil.

6. Return the wrapped pork leg to the smoker and smoke for 6 to 8 hours, or until the internal temperature reaches 205°F.

7. Take the pork leg out of the smoker and keep it covered for about 1 hour. Then unwrap it and carve away.

KNOW YOUR INGREDIENTS: The sugars in the apple juice caramelize as the meat gets cooked. This adds flavor to the bark, and we like that bark.

Smoked German Sausages

SERVES 6

PREP TIME:
10 minutes

SMOKING TIME:
1 hour

TEMPERATURE:
275°F
and 225°F

WOOD:
Beechnut
or cherry

There are just so many great German sausages. I love bratwurst, but you can use just about any thick sausage in this recipe. Make this dish as part of a summer holiday lunch. These sausages, soaked in beer and then seasoned and smoked, have a special flavor. And on top of that, they don't take too long to make. Serve them with your favorite condiments on toasted rolls. I like to use a hard roll instead of a soft hot dog bun. The extra chew just adds to the experience.

12 bratwurst links   ½ cup mustard (any type)

2 (12-ounce) bottles beer,
   at room temperature

1. Preheat the smoker to 275°F.

2. Arrange the brats in a baking dish and pour in the beer.

3. Place the pan in the smoker and cook for 15 minutes. They should start to turn white.

4. Remove the pan from the smoker and reduce the temperature of the smoker to 225°F.

5. Slather the brats with the mustard. Arrange the sausages on a rack and return to the smoker and smoke for 40 minutes, or until the internal temperature reaches 155°F. Be careful not to pop them when testing the temperature.

6. Take the sausages out and serve hot.

KNOW YOUR INGREDIENTS: Use a lighter tasting beer like a pilsner. You can use Dijon, yellow, or whole-grain mustard. All of them will cook off and leave behind a nutty taste.

Smoked Pork with Veggies

SERVES 4

PREP TIME:
20 minutes

SMOKING TIME:
1 hour
30 minutes

TEMPERATURE:
275°F

WOOD:
Apple
or cherry

With the smoked pork and bacon, the sweet and sour flavors in this dish will tantalize your taste buds.

1 pound Brussels sprouts, halved

6 slices bacon

1 teaspoon coarse salt

1 teaspoon freshly ground black pepper

1 tablespoon minced fresh or granulated garlic

1 (3-pound) pork tenderloin, cut into 8 slices

¼ cup olive oil

2 tablespoons Pork Rub (page 165)

½ cup Bacon-Flavored BBQ Sauce (page 170)

2 tablespoons apple cider vinegar

½ cup maple syrup

1. Preheat the smoker to 275°F.

2. Place the halved Brussels sprouts on a sheet pan.

3. In a skillet on the stovetop over medium heat, fry the bacon until half cooked. Take it out of the pan and cut it into pieces. Add the bacon with the pan drippings to the Brussels sprouts. Sprinkle with the salt, pepper, and garlic and toss to mix.

4. Pat the pork slices dry with some paper towels. Brush them with the olive oil and rub them with the pork rub.

5. Place the pork slices in the smoker with the pan of Brussels sprouts underneath. Smoke for 45 minutes.

6. Brush the pork with the BBQ sauce. Add the vinegar and maple syrup to the pan of Brussels sprouts and mix them together.

7. Smoke for another 45 minutes, or until the internal temperature of the pork reaches 145°F.

8. Let the pork rest for 10 minutes. Then cut the pork into 1½-inch pieces and mix it up with the Brussels sprouts. Serve immediately.

Pernil-Style Smoked Pork

SERVES 8

PREP TIME:
6 hours

SMOKING TIME:
6 hours

TEMPERATURE:
250°F

WOOD:
Apple
or cherry

In Spain and parts of Latin America, particularly Puerto Rico, the Dominican Republic, and Cuba, this dish is called pernil. Everyone has their own way of making pernil. In Spain, the word *pernil* also refers to a type of cured ham. Sherry (*jerez* in Spanish) is used a lot in Spanish cuisine, not only for pork and beef, but also in paella, where it's matched with seafood, pork sausage, and chicken. The sherry gives the pork a sweet flair.

3 cups water

¼ cup coarse salt

¼ cup light brown sugar, plus 2 teaspoons

2 cups ice cubes

2 tablespoons apple cider vinegar

6 tablespoons sherry, dry or sweet, divided

1 (8-pound) bone-in pork shoulder

4 tablespoons olive oil

½ cup Pork Rub (page 165)

2 tablespoons minced garlic

2 teaspoons dried oregano

1 teaspoon dried sage

1 teaspoon dried thyme

1 teaspoon freshly ground black pepper

1. In a medium pot, heat the water to almost boiling. Add the salt and stir until it's dissolved. Add ¼ cup brown sugar and stir until it's dissolved. Remove the brine from the heat and cool it off with the ice. Add the vinegar and 4 tablespoons sherry.

2. When the brine solution is cool, score the fat side of the pork with a sharp knife, place it in a large zip-top bag, and add the brine. Close the bag, squeezing out all the air. Refrigerate for about 4 hours.

3. Pat the pork dry with paper towels. Leave it out on the counter for 1 hour.

4. Preheat the smoker to 250°F.

5. In a small bowl, mix together 2 tablespoons olive oil, the pork rub, garlic, oregano, sage, thyme, pepper, and the remaining 2 tablespoons sherry and 2 teaspoons brown sugar. Brush the pork with the remaining 2 tablespoons olive oil, then rub the pork rub mixture into the pork, all over.

6. Smoke the pork for 3 hours.

7. Take it out, wrap it in aluminum foil, and return it to the smoker for another 2 hours.

8. Remove the aluminum foil and let it smoke for 1 hour longer, or until the internal temperature reaches 205°F.

9. Let it rest for at least 30 minutes before serving.

SMOKING TIP: If you want more of chew to the pork, smoke it uncovered at 275°F, until the internal temperature reaches 150°F.

Jamaican-Style Jerked Pork

SERVES 6

PREP TIME:
9 hours

SMOKING TIME:
5 hours

TEMPERATURE:
225°F

WOOD:
Hickory or
mesquite

Warm breezes and ice-cold beer are the perfect companions to this dish, inspired by a Caribbean vacay. The Scotch bonnet pepper is named for its resemblance to the Scottish tam-o'-shanter hat. It packs quite a bit of heat under that hat!

1 (4- to 6-pound) boneless pork shoulder, butterflied (see Tip)

6 tablespoons olive oil

1 tablespoon chopped Scotch bonnet pepper

1 tablespoon granulated garlic

2 tablespoons onion powder

2 tablespoons light brown sugar

1 tablespoon dried parsley

2 teaspoons salt

2 teaspoons cayenne pepper

2 teaspoons smoked paprika

1 teaspoon ground allspice

1 teaspoon dried thyme

1 teaspoon freshly ground black pepper

½ teaspoon ground cumin

½ teaspoon ground nutmeg

1. Score the pork shoulder's fat layer and the meat with a sharp knife, then brush it all over with the olive oil.

2. With a sharp knife, poke holes about ½ inch deep all over the pork.

3. In a small bowl, mix together the Scotch bonnet, granulated garlic, onion powder, brown sugar, parsley, salt, cayenne, smoked paprika, allspice, thyme, black pepper, cumin, and nutmeg. Rub the seasoning into the pork. Then cover it in plastic wrap. Refrigerate for 8 hours. Then, let the pork sit at room temperature for 1 hour before smoking.

4. Preheat the smoker to 225°F.

5. Smoke the pork for 3 hours, or until the internal temperature reaches 145°F.

6. Wrap it in aluminum foil and smoke it for 1 hour longer.

7. Unwrap it and cook for 1 more hour.

8. Let it rest for 30 minutes before serving it to your hungry friends.

KNOW YOUR INGREDIENTS: Ask your butcher to trim off some of the fat from the pork shoulder and butterfly it so that it's 1½ inches thick.

Mexican-Style Smoked Carnitas

SERVES 12

PREP TIME:
11 hours

SMOKING TIME:
10 hours

TEMPERATURE:
225°F, 350°F,
and 400°F

WOOD:
Beechnut
or oak

This method of smoking pork shoulder is inspired by Mexican recipes. The citrus marinade goes deep into the meat. It gets nice and crispy at the end, leaving you with the perfect filling for tacos. Note that you must have a pellet smoker for this recipe.

2 cups Pork Rub
  (page 165), divided

1 tablespoon coarse salt

Juice of 2 limes

Juice of 1 orange

4 bay leaves

6 tablespoons olive oil, divided

1 (8-pound) bone-in
  pork shoulder

1 tablespoon dark brown sugar

1 teaspoon chili powder
  or cayenne pepper

1 teaspoon chipotle powder

1 teaspoon ground cumin

1 teaspoon dried oregano

1. In a small bowl, mix together 1 cup pork rub, the salt, lime juice, orange juice, bay leaves, and 2 tablespoons olive oil.

2. Place the pork shoulder in a 2-gallon zip-top bag. Pour the marinade over the pork, seal the bag, and refrigerate for 10 hours.

3. Take the pork out 1 hour before smoking it. Pat it dry with paper towels.

4. Preheat the smoker to 225°F.

5. Brush the pork with 2 tablespoons olive oil. In a small bowl, mix together the remaining 1 cup pork rub, the brown sugar, chili powder, chipotle powder, cumin, and oregano. Rub the mixture into the pork on all sides.

6. Smoke the pork for about 6 hours, or until the internal temperature reaches 165°F.

7. Take the pork out of the smoker and place in a large metal baking dish. Brush the top with the remaining 2 tablespoons olive oil and cover the pork.

8. Increase the smoker's temperature to 350°F and cook the pork for 4 hours, or until it reaches an internal temperature of 205°F.

9. Remove the pork and let it rest for 1 hour. Keep the pan drippings. Shred the pork.

10. Increase the temperature of the smoker to 400°F and preheat a cast-iron skillet. Add 2 tablespoons of the drippings to the skillet and let it get hot. Then add the pork to the skillet and sear until it's browned, about 5 minutes.

11. Serve warm.

KNOW YOUR INGREDIENTS: Sour orange marinade is widely used in Latin American kitchens and is an excellent alternative to the orange and lime juice in this recipe. It's available in many supermarkets, as well as on Amazon.

Smoked Beef
Chili, page 78

Chapter 4

Beef

WHETHER YOU'RE LOOKING FOR JUICY brined meats, party feasts, or low-and-slow stunners, I've got beef recipes for you. You'll find not only brisket and burgers in this chapter, but also rib-eye steaks, tenderloins, and chuck roasts. And if you haven't tried pulled beef yet, you're in for a treat!! I've got classic American BBQ Belt recipes, as well as some inspired by Mexico, the Southwest, and Korean BBQ that are sure to delight. Lay the sauce on these beef favorites or smoke them dry—both are delicious options. And don't be afraid to try the big, smoky taste of mesquite on beef. Whatever you choose, remember to take the time to enjoy the smoke and savor the flavor.

Smoked Beef Brisket

SERVES 6 TO 8

PREP TIME:
15 minutes

SMOKING TIME:
11 to 13 hours

TEMPERATURE:
225°F

WOOD:
Apple,
hickory, or
mesquite

This is a traditional 'cue from the American South and West that's now loved coast to coast and beyond! Get your butcher to trim down your brisket as a "flat cut," on which most of the fat is on the bottom of the brisket, or as a "point cut," on which the fat is marbled.

1 (10- to 12-pound) whole
  beef brisket, fat trimmed
  to a ¼-inch thickness

1 cup Beef Rub (page 166)

1. Preheat the smoker to 225°F.

2. Generously season the brisket all over with the beef rub.

3. Place the brisket fat-side down in the smoker. Insert a thermometer into the thickest part of the meat.

4. Smoke the brisket for 3 to 5 hours, or until it reaches an internal temperature of 160°F.

5. Remove it from the smoker and double-wrap it in butcher paper (preferred) or aluminum foil. Return the brisket to the smoker and cook for as much as another 8 or so hours (see Smoking tip), or until it reaches an internal temperature of 204°F.

6. Remove the brisket, wrap it in a towel, and let it rest for at least 30 minutes before serving.

SMOKING TIP: When you're smoking a big cut low and slow, the most important thing is to get the internal temperature right. If you're smoking on a cold or very windy day, it may take longer. Some temperature controls are more accurate than others, so always have an instant-read food thermometer handy. You also have to contend with the famous stall.

PAIR IT WITH: Enjoy this brisket with Smoked Mac 'n' Cheese (page 120). It's also great for sandwiches with a cold beer.

Reverse-Seared and Smoked Steak

SERVES 2

PREP TIME:
4 hours
30 minutes

SMOKING TIME:
1 hour
30 minutes

TEMPERATURE:
225°F
and 600°F

WOOD:
Hickory
or oak

The reverse sear is one of the best ways to serve a smoked steak; it comes out perfectly medium-rare with an amazing, crispy crust. Remember to always use a meat thermometer. Steak is too pricey for a best guess.

1 (2-pound) rib-eye steak (2 to 2½ inches thick)

3 teaspoons coarse salt, divided

2 tablespoons granulated garlic

1 tablespoon freshly ground black pepper

2 teaspoons olive oil

1. Rub the steak with 1 teaspoon salt on both sides. Cover it tightly with plastic wrap and refrigerate for 4 hours.

2. Wipe the salt off the steak and let it come to room temperature. It should take about 30 minutes.

3. Preheat the smoker to 225°F and fill the water pan.

4. In a small bowl, mix together the garlic, pepper, and remaining 2 teaspoons salt. Brush the steak all over with the olive oil. Then, generously sprinkle the garlic mixture on both sides of the steak.

5. Smoke the steak for 1 hour 30 minutes, or until the internal temperature reaches 100°F Check it after the first hour.

6. If you have a pellet smoker with a searing feature that gets you above 600°F, crank it up. Otherwise, heat a cast-iron skillet over high heat on the stovetop.

7. Give the meat a good sear, 2 to 4 minutes per side, until the internal temperature reaches 125°F for rare or 135°F for medium.

8. To keep the steak juicy, let it rest for 10 minutes before serving.

KNOW YOUR INGREDIENTS: I love rib eye, but a couple of New York strips are also a good choice.

Smoked Meat Loaf

SERVES 4

PREP TIME:
20 minutes

SMOKING TIME:
3 hours

TEMPERATURE:
250°F

WOOD:
Hickory,
pecan, or oak

Meat loaf is a quintessential North American dinner. The dish has its roots in Pennsylvania Dutch cooking, which calls for slowly smoking in a wood-burning oven. Nowadays, meat loaf recipes have been widely adapted to the smoker.

1 tablespoon olive oil

2 cups diced red onions

4 garlic cloves, thinly sliced

2 slices bread

2 large eggs, lightly beaten

¾ cup beef stock

1 tablespoon
Worcestershire sauce

2 pounds ground beef
(80% lean)

1 teaspoon granulated garlic

1 teaspoon dried parsley

1 teaspoon dried thyme

1 teaspoon coarse salt

3 teaspoons freshly ground
black pepper, divided

½ cup ketchup

½ cup packed light brown sugar

1. Preheat the smoker to 250°F and fill the water pan.

2. In a skillet on the stovetop, heat the olive oil over medium-high heat. Add the onions and cook for about 5 minutes, or until they start to turn translucent. Add the sliced garlic during the last minute. Let cool slightly.

3. Put the bread in a food processor and pulse to make coarse bread crumbs. Place the crumbs in a large bowl. Add the beaten eggs, beef stock, Worcestershire sauce, and fried onions and garlic. Toss the mixture very lightly, just enough to coat the bread crumbs. Add the ground beef, granulated garlic, parsley, thyme, salt, and 1 teaspoon pepper. Mix it all up lightly, leaving it coarse.

4. Dump the mixture onto a strip of wax paper long enough to fit the loaf with some extra at each end for "handles." Form the mixture into a loaf shape, then put it (with the wax paper) into a loaf pan.

5. In a small bowl, whisk together the ketchup, brown sugar, and remaining 2 teaspoons pepper. Pour half of the glaze over the meat loaf.

6. Smoke the meat loaf for 3 hours, or until the internal temperature reaches 165°F.

7. Remove the meat loaf and pour the rest of the glaze over it. Let it rest for 10 minutes before serving.

KNOW YOUR INGREDIENTS: You can also use ground chuck.

Smoked Steak Fajitas

SERVES 6

PREP TIME:
4 hours

SMOKING TIME:
3 hours

TEMPERATURE:
225°F
and 550°F

WOOD:
Hickory
or oak

This Tex-Mex favorite pleases everybody and feeds a crowd. To complete the experience, serve the fajitas with bowls of tomato salsa, guacamole, and sour cream. You can also wrap some torti- llas in aluminum foil and smoke them for the last 30 minutes with the steak and veggies.

¾ cup Basic Beef
Marinade (page 169)

6 tablespoons tequila

¼ cup Beef Rub (page 166)

1 teaspoon cayenne
pepper (optional)

1 tablespoon granulated garlic

2 pounds skirt steak

2 large yellow or red
onions, cut into rings

3 red or green bell peppers,
cut into ½-inch rings

2 tablespoons olive oil

1. In a small bowl, mix together the beef marinade, tequila, beef rub, cayenne (if using), and garlic.

2. Place the steak in a nonaluminum dish, large enough so that the meat lies flat. Cover both sides with the marinade. Cover the dish and refrigerate the steak for 4 hours, turning it every hour.

3. Preheat the smoker to 225°F.

4. Transfer the steak to a large ovenproof glass dish and pour the marinade over it.

5. Smoke the steak for 1 hour and 30 minutes. Place the onions and peppers on a grill mat or wire grill screen and drizzle the olive oil over them. Smoke them, along with the steak, for another 1 hour and 30 minutes. When the steak reaches an internal temperature of 100°F, it is ready for a quick sea

6. If you're using a pellet smoker, increase the temperature to 550°F and cook the steak for 10 to 12 minutes, or until the internal temperature reaches 130°F for medium-rare. If

not, heat a cast-iron skillet on the stovetop over high heat. Sear the steak for 2 to 3 minutes per side, brushing it with the extra smoked marinade, bringing the steak to 135°F for medium.

7. Let the steak rest for 10 minutes, then slice it across the grain, with the knife at a 45-degree angle to the cutting board, into thin strips. Place it on the serving platter with the onions and peppers.

SMOKING TIP: The *vaqueros* would probably use mesquite out on the range. That heavy smoky flavor would make them feel right at home.

Smoked Philly-Style Sandwiches

SERVES 4

PREP TIME:
30 minutes

SMOKING TIME:
1 hour

TEMPERATURE:
275°F

WOOD:
Hickory

If you can't find already-shaved prime rib or sirloin, pass frozen meat through a food processor with the slicing disc.

1½ pounds prime rib or sirloin, shaved into very thin slices

6 tablespoons olive oil, plus more for drizzling

1 teaspoon coarse salt

1 teaspoon freshly ground black pepper

2 teaspoons garlic powder

1 teaspoon onion powder

1 pound onions, sliced

1 pound green bell peppers, cut into thin strips

1 tablespoon Beef Rub (page 166)

8 ounces mushrooms, sliced

4 tablespoons cheddar cheese spread or Cheez Whiz

4 kaiser rolls, split and toasted

8 slices provolone cheese

1. Season the beef slices with 2 tablespoons olive oil, the salt, pepper, garlic powder, and onion powder. Toss to combine.

2. Preheat the smoker to 275°F.

3. Place the meat on a perforated BBQ skillet and set it on a rack in the smoker.

4. Place the onions and bell peppers in a baking dish. Add the remaining 4 tablespoons olive oil and the beef rub. Mix it all up, then place it in the smoker under the beef.

5. Smoke the beef and veggies for 1 hour, or until the internal temperature of the beef reaches 135°F.

6. During the last 5 minutes of smoking, warm a drizzle of olive oil in a skillet on the stovetop over medium heat and fry the mushrooms.

7. For each sandwich, spread 1 tablespoon of cheese spread onto the bottom half of a roll. Top with a slice of provolone and then the meat, onions, peppers, mushrooms, and a second slice of provolone. Close up the sandwich and serve warm.

Texas-Style Smoked Beef Short Ribs

SERVES 4

PREP TIME:
8 hours

SMOKING TIME:
5 to 8 hours

TEMPERATURE:
225°F

WOOD:
Hickory, oak,
or pecan

Plate ribs are the authentic Texas-size beef ribs. They're good to have and hard to get. Chuck ribs are better for individual portions. Either way, ask your butcher to trim them. For this recipe, low and slow is the way to go.

1 tablespoon coarse salt

8 pounds chuck or plate ribs, trimmed of fat and membrane

¾ cup plus 2 tablespoons Beef Rub (page 166)

2 tablespoons light brown sugar

2 teaspoons chipotle powder

2 tablespoons olive oil

1 tablespoon molasses

1 cup apple juice

1. Sprinkle the salt over the ribs. Wrap them in plastic wrap and refrigerate overnight.

2. Preheat the smoker to 225°F.

3. Pat the ribs dry with paper towels, removing any excess salt.

4. In a small bowl, mix together the beef rub, brown sugar, chipotle powder, olive oil, and molasses. Rub that paste onto the ribs.

5. Place the ribs in the smoker meat-side up. Smoke for 3 hours. Fill a spray bottle with apple juice.

6. Spray them with the apple juice and smoke for another 2 hours, spritzing again with the juice every hour, or until the internal temperature reaches 205°F. Be prepared to cook them for another couple of hours if the internal temperature stalls.

7. Let them rest for 10 minutes before serving.

SMOKING TIP: If you want the ribs to be more tender, spritz them with apple juice after the first 3 hours of cooking. Then, wrap them in butcher paper or aluminum foil and cook them for another 2 hours. Then unwrap the ribs, spray them again, and smoke them unwrapped for 1 hour.

Smoked Beef Chili

SERVES 6

PREP TIME:
30 minutes

SMOKING TIME:
2 hours

TEMPERATURE:
250°F

WOOD:
Hickory or
mesquite

Chili con carne came to the American Southwest from Mexico more than 175 years ago. This version, with smoky ground beef and plenty of spices, will be a serious upgrade from your normal chili.

2 pounds ground chuck

2 teaspoons chili powder

2 teaspoons paprika

2 teaspoons coarse salt

1 teaspoon ancho powder
 or red pepper flakes

1 teaspoon chipotle powder

1 teaspoon ground cumin

1 teaspoon garlic powder

1 teaspoon onion powder

1 teaspoon dried oregano

1 teaspoon freshly ground
 black pepper

1 large red onion, diced

1 red bell pepper, chopped

1 green bell pepper, chopped

2 tablespoons minced garlic

2 tablespoons olive oil

1 (28-ounce) can
 crushed tomatoes

½ cup tomato paste

1 (16-ounce) can pinto beans,
 drained and rinsed

1 (16-ounce) can kidney
 beans, drained and rinsed

2 cups beef broth

1. Preheat the smoker to 250°F.

2. In a large bowl, combine the ground chuck, chili powder, paprika, salt, ancho powder, chipotle powder, cumin, garlic powder, onion powder, oregano, and black pepper. Mix thoroughly.

3. In the bottom of a large baking dish, spread the onions, bell peppers, and minced garlic. Drizzle the olive oil over them.

4. Place the ground beef in a perforated BBQ skillet and set it in the smoker. Place the baking dish with the vegetables under the skillet. Smoke for 1 hour, breaking up the burger as it cooks.

5. Stir the crushed tomatoes and tomato paste into the vegetables in the baking dish. Then add the pinto beans, kidney beans, smoked ground beef, and beef broth. Stir to combine.

6. Smoke for 1 more hour, stirring every 20 minutes.

7. Serve warm.

PAIR IT WITH: This smoked Beef Chili is delicious in burritos. If you're feeling indulgent, add Smoked Corn Salsa (page 134).

Korean-Style Short Ribs

SERVES 4

PREP TIME:
5 hours

SMOKING TIME:
3 hours
30 minutes

TEMPERATURE:
225°F

WOOD:
Beechnut,
cherry, or oak

This recipe is inspired by Korean BBQ. I like to use short ribs, cut thin (about 1½ inches) across the rib bones, called "cross-cut short ribs" or "flanken-style." If you have a Korean grocery store or butcher, they will know what you're looking for.

6 cups cold water

1 tablespoon coarse salt

2 pounds cross-cut or
  flanken-style short ribs

7 tablespoons soy sauce

¼ cup rice wine

¼ cup packed light brown sugar

3 tablespoons minced garlic

1 teaspoon grated fresh ginger

1 teaspoon freshly ground
  black pepper

½ teaspoon cayenne or red
  pepper flakes (optional)

½ cup apple juice

2 tablespoons apple jelly

1. In a large bowl, combine the water and salt and stir to dissolve. Add the short ribs and let soak for 30 minutes. Remove the ribs and pat dry with paper towels.

2. In a small bowl, mix together the soy sauce, rice wine, brown sugar, garlic, ginger, black pepper, and cayenne (if using) to make the marinade.

3. Place the ribs in a large zip-top bag and pour the marinade over them. Squeeze the air out of the bag, seal it, and refrigerate the ribs for 4 hours.

4. Take the ribs out of the bag and dry them with paper towels. Let them come to room temperature, about 30 minutes.

5. Preheat the smoker to 225°F.

6. Smoke the ribs for 2 hours.

7. Meanwhile, in a bowl, mix the apple juice and jelly.

8. Brush the ribs with the apple mixture and smoke for another 1 hour 30 minutes, or until the internal temperature reaches 195°F. Baste the ribs with the apple mixture every hour.

9. Serve warm.

KNOW YOUR INGREDIENTS: You can substitute rice vinegar or cider vinegar for the rice wine. The sugars in the apple jelly not only caramelize to make a good bark, they make the ribs a little sticky, too.

Bacon-Wrapped Beef Tenderloin

SERVES 8

PREP TIME:
15 minutes

SMOKING TIME:
1 hour
30 minutes

TEMPERATURE:
250°F

WOOD:
Apple,
hickory,
or maple

Beef tenderloin is just another way to say filet mignon. These bacon-wrapped filets make an excellent dish for a sit-down dinner party. And on top of that, it's a fast dinner, as smoking meat goes.

1 (5- to 6-pound) beef tenderloin

2 tablespoons olive oil

½ cup Beef Rub (page 166)

12 to 14 slices bacon

½ cup Bacon-Flavored BBQ Sauce (page 170)

1. Preheat the smoker to 250°F.

2. Pat the tenderloin dry with paper towels. Then brush the meat with the olive oil and sprinkle the beef rub over all sides, rubbing it into the meat.

3. Cut a piece of wax paper that's the length of the tenderloin. Place the bacon slices on the wax paper so that they are slightly overlapping along the edges. Then set the tenderloin across the bacon strips at one end. Slowly and carefully, begin to roll the tenderloin. You can use toothpicks to help fasten the bacon to the beef, if needed.

4. Smoke the tenderloin for 1 hour.

5. Remove the tenderloin and brush it with the BBQ sauce. Continue to smoke for 30 minutes, or until the internal temperature reaches 135°F.

6. Let the tenderloin rest for 10 minutes before serving.

SMOKING TIP: If you are using a pellet smoker and would like the bacon to be crispier, increase the temperature to 400°F after you brush the BBQ sauce over the bacon and cook for 10 to 12 minutes.

Smoked Burnt Ends of Brisket

SERVES 6

PREP TIME:
20 minutes

SMOKING TIME:
8 hours

TEMPERATURE:
250°F

WOOD:
Hickory,
mesquite,
or pecan

Burnt ends come from the fatty point of the beef brisket, which is about half of the cut. Smoking the fatty point gives you caramelized chunks of meat so full of flavor that you'll want to make a double batch.

½ cup Beef Rub (page 166)

2 tablespoons molasses

4 tablespoons light brown sugar, divided

1 teaspoon freshly ground black pepper

1 (6- to 8-pound) fatty point of beef brisket

½ cup olive oil

1 cup Bacon-Flavored BBQ Sauce (page 170)

1. Preheat the smoker to 250°F.

2. In a small bowl, mix together the beef rub, molasses, 2 tablespoons brown sugar, and the pepper. Brush the brisket with the olive oil, then rub the paste into the meat.

3. Smoke the brisket for 6 hours, or until the internal temperature reaches 195°F.

4. Take the brisket out of the smoker and let it rest for 15 minutes.

5. Cut the brisket into 1½-inch chunks and place them in a baking dish. Add the BBQ sauce and remaining 2 tablespoons brown sugar. Mix it all up to coat the brisket.

6. Place the baking dish in the smoker and smoke for 2 more hours, stirring every 30 minutes.

7. Serve hot.

KNOW YOUR INGREDIENTS: You can substitute maple syrup for the molasses and brown sugar. And if you want it to be spicier, add 1 teaspoon of cayenne pepper to the BBQ sauce.

Smoked Beef Jerky

SERVES 4

PREP TIME:
2 hours

SMOKING TIME:
2 hours
30 minutes

TEMPERATURE:
225°F

WOOD:
Alder,
cherry,
hickory,
or oak

Dried and spiced beef jerky is great in cowboy-style beans, with eggs in the morning, or as a snack any time of day. It can also be used as a main dish for folks living that Paleo life.

1 pound London broil (such as top round)

½ cup apple cider vinegar

¼ cup beef broth

¼ cup Beef Rub (page 166)

2 tablespoons blackstrap molasses

1 tablespoon light brown sugar

1. Trim the fat from the meat, then cut it into strips that are about ¼ inch thick. It's easier to cut when the meat is very cold.

2. In a small bowl, mix together the vinegar, broth, beef rub, molasses, and brown sugar. Place the strips of beef in a glass dish (do not use an aluminum pan). Pour the marinade over the beef strips, making sure they are coated. Refrigerate for 2 hours.

3. Preheat the smoker to 225°F.

4. Pat the beef strips dry with paper towels.

5. Place the beef strips in the smoker, making sure there is space between the strips. Smoke for 2 hours 30 minutes, or until the meat is firm and the internal temperatures reaches 150°F.

6. Take the strips out of the smoker and let them rest for 10 minutes before enjoying.

SMOKING TIP: In the last 30 minutes of smoking, open the smoker's vents to increase the air flowing into it. This helps dry the jerky and make it firmer. If you want your jerky even firmer, don't marinate it; just apply the beef rub.

Smoked Tri-Tip

SERVES 4

PREP TIME:
15 minutes

SMOKING TIME:
2 hours

TEMPERATURE:
225°F

WOOD:
Hickory, oak,
or pecan

Tri-tips come from the lower part of the sirloin that's shaped like a triangle. I recommend getting your tri-tip trimmed, without the fat. I have heard that tri-tips were popular in the American West before they became a thing all over the country.

1 (2- to 3-pound) tri-tip

1 tablespoon olive oil

1 tablespoon coarse salt

1 tablespoon freshly
ground black pepper

2 tablespoons granulated garlic

1 cup Bacon-Flavored BBQ
Sauce (page 170), divided

2 tablespoons unsalted butter

1 rosemary sprig

1. Preheat the smoker to 225°F.

2. Brush the meat with the olive oil and generously sprinkle with the salt, pepper, and garlic.

3. Smoke the meat for 1 hour 30 minutes.

4. Remove the trip-tip, brush it with ½ cup BBQ sauce, then smoke for another 30 minutes, or until the internal temperature reaches 110°F. Remove the meat from the smoker.

5. In a cast-iron skillet on the stovetop, melt the butter over high heat until it's sizzling. Add the sprig of rosemary. Sear the meat on both sides for 3 to 4 minutes per side. The internal temperature should reach 125°F for rare and 135°F for medium.

6. Let the tri-tip rest for 15 minutes before slicing. The grain of tri-tip meat changes, so to slice, start at the smallest tip and cut against the grain.

7. Serve the tri-tip with the remaining ½ cup BBQ sauce.

SMOKING TIP: This cut of meat can stand up to a stronger smoke. If you want more of the Southwestern ranch flavor, use mesquite. It's the wood that cowboys would use.

Smoked Pulled Beef Sandwiches

SERVES 6

PREP TIME:
12 hours

SMOKING TIME:
6 hours

TEMPERATURE:
225°F

WOOD:
Hickory, oak,
or pecan

My first love is my wife, my second love is the pulled pork sandwich, and my third is this pulled beef sandwich. Pulled beef sandwiches made from smoked chuck roast are in the same superstar league as brisket and pulled pork, so don't sleep on this recipe!

2 (3-pound) boneless chuck roasts, at least 2 inches thick

¾ cup Beef Rub (page 166)

1 tablespoon light brown sugar

1 teaspoon cayenne pepper

3 tablespoons olive oil

½ cup apple juice

1 cup Bacon-Flavored BBQ Sauce (page 170), divided

6 brioche buns, split and toasted

6 lettuce leaves

1. Pat the roasts dry with paper towels.

2. In a small bowl, mix together the beef rub, brown sugar, and cayenne. Brush the roasts all over with the olive oil and rub on all sides with the seasoning mixture. Refrigerate the roasts, uncovered, for 8 to 12 hours.

3. Take the chuck roasts out of the fridge and bring to room temperature, about 45 minutes.

4. Preheat the smoker to 225°F. Fill a spray bottle with apple juice.

5. Smoke the roasts for about 3 hours, or until the internal temperature reaches 180°F.

6. Take the roasts out, spray them with the apple juice, and wrap them in butcher paper or foil. Return them to the smoker and cook for another 1 hour 30 minutes.

7. Take the roasts out of the smoker and unwrap them. Baste them with ½ cup BBQ sauce and return them to the smoker. Smoke for another 1 hour 30 minutes, or until the internal

temperature reaches 210°F. The meat should be very tender, so that it has little resistance to a knife.

8. Remove the roasts, let them rest for 15 minutes, and then shred them.

9. On each bottom brioche bun, place a leaf of lettuce. Spoon some pulled beef onto the sandwiches, top with the remaining ½ cup BBQ sauce, and serve.

KNOW YOUR INGREDIENTS: I like brioche buns for this recipe, but a sub roll cut in half does the trick, too. Feel free to top with a couple slices of provolone.

Smoked Pot Roast

SERVES 6

PREP TIME:
15 minutes

SMOKING TIME:
5 hours
30 minutes

TEMPERATURE:
190°F
and 275°F

WOOD:
Beechnut,
cherry,
or hickory

There's nothing like a comforting pot roast when the temperature drops. Chuck roast comes from the shoulder of beef, so it's a little like smoking brisket. This recipe gives you a good reason to use your smoker when it's cold outside.

1 (3- to 4-pound) beef chuck roast

2 tablespoons olive oil

2 teaspoons coarse salt

2 teaspoons freshly ground black pepper

1 teaspoon cayenne pepper

2 teaspoons granulated garlic

2 teaspoons onion powder

1½ pounds fingerling or small potatoes, halved

1½ pounds carrots, cut into 1½- to 2-inch pieces

1 pound pearl onions, peeled

2 rosemary sprigs

1 tablespoon chipotle powder

1 cup red wine

2 cups beef broth

1. Preheat the smoker to 190°F.

2. Pat the chuck roast with paper towels to dry it. Brush the roast with the olive oil, then sprinkle the salt, pepper, cayenne, garlic, and onion powder over all sides of the meat.

3. Smoke the roast for 1 hour 30 minutes.

4. Put the potatoes, carrots, onions, rosemary, and chipotle powder in a Dutch oven or baking dish that you can cover with aluminum foil. Pour the wine and beef broth over the vegetables and spices.

5. Take the chuck roast out of the smoker and place it over the vegetables, then cover the dish.

6. Increase the smoker temperature to 275°F. Place the Dutch oven or covered baking dish in the smoker and cook for another 4 hours, or until the internal temperature of the meat reaches 165°F.

7. Serve warm.

Smoked Maple-Bacon Cheeseburgers

SERVES 6

PREP TIME:
15 minutes

SMOKING TIME:
1 hour

TEMPERATURE:
225°F

WOOD:
Apple or
cherry/
hickory mix

Grilled burgers are a classic of American backyard cookouts. But when you smoke the burgers and add candied bacon and cheese, you get a burger unlike any other. I promise it's worth the extra time.

12 ground beef patties (80% lean, 4 ounces each)	6 large burger buns, split and toasted
1 tablespoon coarse salt	12 slices cheese of your choice
1 tablespoon coarsely ground black pepper	12 slices Smoked Candied Bacon (page 57)
1 tablespoon granulated garlic	6 slices tomato
12 leaves lettuce	6 slices onion

1. Preheat the smoker to 225°F.

2. Season the patties with the salt, pepper, and granulated garlic.

3. Smoke the burgers for 1 hour, or until their internal temperature reaches 145°F.

4. To build the burgers, place with a layer of lettuce on the bottom of each bun. Place a patty over the lettuce, then a slice of cheese on top, then 2 slices of candied bacon, crisscrossed. Add another patty, another slice of cheese, and a slice each of tomato and onion.

5. Serve the burgers on a big serving board.

> **SMOKING TIP:** If you have a pellet smoker, set the temperature to 400°F and smoke the burgers for 20 minutes (check them after 15 minutes, to be safe). Note, however, that the burgers will not be as smoky with so little time in the smoker. If you want a stronger smoke taste, use mesquite wood.

Mesquite-Smoked Barbacoa

SERVES 4

PREP TIME:
7 hours

SMOKING TIME:
5 to 7 hours

TEMPERATURE:
225°F

WOOD:
Mesquite

This recipe comes from Northern Mexico and the American Southwest, but barbacoa is thought to have originated in Barbados. Barbacoa-style cooking still refers to cooking meat over an open fire or, even more traditionally, in a fire pit covered with succulent leaves. Now that's something to try! Barbacoa is tender perfection, since it cooks low and slow. I love the hits of spice from all the peppers.

1 (3-pound) bone-in beef chuck roast

¼ cup Beef Rub (page 166)

1 tablespoon light brown sugar

2 tablespoons minced garlic

2 teaspoons chopped jalapeño

1 teaspoon ancho powder or red pepper flakes

1 teaspoon chipotle powder

1 teaspoon coarsely ground black pepper

1 teaspoon ground cumin

1 teaspoon ground cinnamon

1 cup bitter orange juice (also called Seville orange juice)

1 teaspoon chopped fresh oregano

1 tablespoon chopped fresh cilantro

1 teaspoon olive oil

1 teaspoon salt

1 teaspoon cayenne pepper

2 teaspoons granulated garlic

½ cup Bacon-Flavored BBQ Sauce (page 170)

1 tablespoon fresh lime juice

1. With a sharp knife, trim the fat off the side of the roast. Don't leave more than ¼ inch.

2. In a large bowl or container with a cover, combine the beef rub, brown sugar, minced garlic, jalapeño, ancho powder, chipotle powder, black pepper, cumin, and cinnamon. Mix in the orange juice, oregano, and cilantro.

3. Place the meat in the container and coat it completely. Refrigerate for 7 hours.

4. Preheat the smoker to 225°F.

5. Remove the meat from the marinade and pat it dry with paper towels.

6. Brush the olive oil over the roast and then sprinkle the salt, cayenne, and granulated garlic on all sides.

7. Smoke the chuck roast for 3 to 5 hours, or until the internal temperature reaches 145°F.

8. Remove the roast, cover in aluminum foil, return to the smoker and smoke for 1 more hour.

9. Remove it again, take off the foil, and smoke it for 30 more minutes.

10. While the roast is smoking, mix the BBQ sauce with the lime juice. Baste the roast, then cook for 30 more minutes, still unwrapped.

11. Serve warm.

SMOKING TIP: If the mesquite is too strong of a smoke for your taste, use hickory or oak.

Stuffed and Smoked Burgers

SERVES 6

PREP TIME:
45 minutes

SMOKING TIME:
1 hour

TEMPERATURE:
275°F

WOOD:
Hickory

Served on a board covered in crispy French fries, these burgers will make your friends say, "Wowza!" The best part is that you can customize each burger with the stuffing of their choice. In order to prepare this recipe, you will need a burger stuffer-press, which you can get from Amazon or Walmart.

1 hot dog

1 teaspoon olive oil

4 ounces sliced mushrooms

3 tablespoons crumbled
blue cheese

¼ cup crumbled cooked bacon

1 (8-ounce) jar caramelized
red onion chutney

3 tablespoons shredded
pepper Jack cheese

Cooking spray

2¼ pounds ground
beef (80% lean)

2 tablespoons coarse salt

2 tablespoons freshly
ground black pepper

¼ cup granulated garlic

6 large burger buns,
split and toasted

Burger condiments and
toppings of choice

1. Preheat the smoker to 275°F.

2. Slice the hot dog lengthwise. In a frying pan over medium heat, warm 1 teaspoon olive oil and sear the hot dog on both sides. Then, remove it from the heat and cut it into ½-inch pieces.

3. Place the hot dog pieces, sliced mushrooms, blue cheese, bacon, onion chutney, and pepper Jack all in their own separate bowls to make a "stuffing bar."

4. Mist the burger press with cooking spray. To make each burger, take 4 ounces ground beef and place it in the press, pressing it onto the bottom and sides. Fill the burger with 3 tablespoons of the toppings of your choice. Then form the top of the burger with another 2 ounces meat. Seal the

top layer and sides of the meat together, pressing with your fingers. Flip the burger out of the mold and onto a tray lined with wax paper. Repeat to make a total of 6 burgers.

5. Sprinkle the burgers with the salt, pepper, and granulated garlic.

6. Smoke the burgers for 1 hour, or until the internal temperature reaches 165°F.

7. Let the burgers rest for 10 minutes. Serve the burgers on the buns topped with your favorite condiments and toppings.

KNOW YOUR INGREDIENTS: Make a pizza burger by using 1 tablespoon of pizza sauce, 1 tablespoon of shredded mozzarella, and 1 tablespoon of grated Parmesan for the stuffing.

Canadian-Style
Smoked Salmon on
Cedar, page 99

Chapter 5

Fish and Shellfish

SEAFOOD GIVES A WHOLE DIFFERENT feeling and taste to smoking. Its lighter meat allows it to soak up spices like a sponge, and it requires much less cooking, brining, and marinating time than other proteins. This means you get fresh, delicious fish in a flash. Additionally, there are so many different tastes and textures to seafood. From the dense, sweet flesh of a smoked lobster to the delicate flakes of a smoked sea bass, you'll be sure to find your new favorite meal in this chapter. Once again, this chapter is a nice tour of the United States, with recipes from the Pacific Northwest, the Gulf of Mexico, and New England, as well as from my homeland, the Canadian Maritimes. Both the finfish and shellfish recipes tend to use lighter-tasting woods to let the fresh flavors of the seafood take center stage. However, you can always test out different woods to suit your palate and experiment with different sauces and spices to liven up the recipes. Just don't forget the lemon wedges!

Spicy Smoked Tuna Tacos

SERVES 4

PREP TIME:
5 hours

SMOKING TIME:
1 hour

TEMPERATURE:
250°F

WOOD:
Apple
or cherry

This is a great summer dish for eating by the side of the smoker and keeping company with the 'cue master. The tuna comes out moist and flaky with a warm, rich flavor from the smoke. And everyone makes their own!

3 tablespoons Fish Rub (page 167)

2 tablespoons olive oil

1 tablespoon minced garlic

Salt

Freshly cracked black pepper

2 (5-ounce) tuna steaks, about 1¼ inches thick

1 tablespoon red pepper flakes

1 (14-ounce) bag coleslaw mix

1 cup cubed fresh pineapple

1½ cups poppy seed dressing

4 (8-inch) flour tortillas

1 cup cilantro-lime dressing

2 limes, cut into quarters

1. In a small bowl, combine the fish rub, olive oil, garlic, and salt and pepper to taste. Rub both sides of the steaks with the mixture. Place the tuna in a plastic zip-top bag and refrigerate for 5 hours.

2. Preheat the smoker to 250°F.

3. Take the tuna out of the bag and sprinkle the red pepper flakes on both sides.

4. Smoke the tuna for about 1 hour, or until the internal temperature reaches 140°F.

5. Meanwhile, in a large bowl, toss together the slaw mix, pineapple, and poppy seed dressing.

6. Wrap the tortillas in aluminum foil and place them on a smoker rack to keep them warm.

7. Place the cooked tuna on a cutting board and cut it into ½-inch slices.

8. For each taco, add a couple tablespoons of coleslaw, a couple slices of grilled tuna, and then another couple tablespoons of coleslaw. Drizzle the cilantro-lime dressing over the taco.

9. Serve warm with limes for squeezing.

PAIR IT WITH: These are wonderful with a side of Bacon-Wrapped Asparagus (page 124).

Bacon-Wrapped Smoked Scallops

SERVES 6

PREP TIME:
1 hour
30 minutes

SMOKING TIME:
1 hour

TEMPERATURE:
225°F

WOOD:
Alder, apple,
or cherry

I'll take any chance I get to wrap stuff in bacon, and seafood is no exception. The fresh taste of the ocean, a tangy marinade, and the saltiness of the bacon is pure delight.

½ cup olive oil

2 tablespoons fresh lime juice

2 teaspoons minced garlic

2 teaspoons chopped
fresh cilantro

1 teaspoon salt

1 teaspoon freshly ground
black pepper

24 sea scallops (about
2 pounds)

24 slices bacon

1 lemon, cut into wedges

1. In a bowl, mix together the olive oil, lime juice, garlic, cilantro, salt, and pepper. Add the scallops and toss to coat them completely. Cover the bowl and refrigerate for about 1 hour.

2. Preheat the smoker to 225°F. If using wooden skewers, soak them in water for at least 30 minutes.

3. Wrap a scallop with a piece of bacon, going around twice, and run a skewer through it. Repeat with the remaining scallops and bacon so that each skewer has 4 scallops on it.

4. Transfer the marinade to a small saucepan on the stovetop over medium heat and boil for 5 minutes, then set it aside.

5. Smoke the skewers, turning frequently, for 45 minutes to 1 hour, or until the internal temperature reaches 145°F. Each time you turn the skewers, brush them with the reserved marinade.

6. Serve immediately with the lemon wedges.

KNOW YOUR INGREDIENTS: You can substitute parsley for the cilantro. Don't substitute bay scallops for the sea scallops; they're too small and cook faster than the bacon.

Canadian-Style Smoked Salmon on Cedar

SERVES 6

PREP TIME:
5 hours

SMOKING TIME:
40 minutes

TEMPERATURE:
250°F

WOOD:
Alder

Smoking salmon on cedar planks is a traditional practice in Canada and the American Pacific Northwest. Try serving this smoky-sweet fish with red onions, capers, or cream cheese on a bagel.

1½ cups maple sugar

½ cup coarse salt

2 tablespoons Fish Rub (page 167)

1 tablespoon freshly ground black pepper

2 teaspoons grated lemon zest

2 (1½- to 2-pound) skin-on salmon fillets

¾ cup maple syrup, divided

2 untreated cedar planks

2 teaspoons chopped fresh parsley

1. In a bowl, mix together the maple sugar, salt, fish rub, pepper, and lemon zest. Season the salmon on both sides with the mixture, then drizzle ½ cup maple syrup over the flesh side of each fillet.

2. Wrap the fillets in plastic wrap and refrigerate for 4 hours.

3. Rinse the fish under cold water to remove the rub. Pat dry with paper towels and let the fillets air-dry in a cool place for 1 hour.

4. At the same time, soak the cedar planks for 1 hour.

5. Preheat the smoker to 250°F.

6. Set the planks inside the smoker. Wait until they start to crack or smoke a little, then take them out, using your BBQ mitts. Place the fish on the planks skin-side down, then return the fish-topped planks to the smoker.

7. Smoke the fish for 25 minutes.

8. Baste the fillets lightly with the remaining ¼ cup maple syrup and continue to smoke for another 15 minutes, or until the internal temperature reaches 140°F.

9. Let the salmon rest for 10 minutes, then garnish with the parsley and serve.

Smoked Seafood Pizza

SERVES 4

PREP TIME:
40 minutes

SMOKING TIME:
18 to
23 minutes

TEMPERATURE:
450°F

WOOD:
Apple, cherry,
or maple

Pizza with a smoky taste is a good reason to have a pellet smoker. Once you make a thin-crust pizza in a smoker, you'll never want an oven-baked one again. If you don't have a pizza stone, a cast-iron skillet will do in a pinch. And the best way to get the pizza dough onto the pizza stone is with a pizza peel, a long-handled wooden shovel.

2 tablespoons olive oil

2 tablespoons minced garlic

1 teaspoon chopped
fresh cilantro

1 teaspoon coarse salt

1 teaspoon freshly ground
black pepper

1½ pounds large shrimp,
peeled and deveined

½ cup cornmeal

1 pound pizza dough,
store-bought or your
favorite recipe

2 cups store-bought
Alfredo sauce

1 teaspoon red pepper flakes

8 ounces mozzarella
cheese, shredded

4 ounces Parmesan
cheese, grated

1. Preheat a pellet smoker to 450°F. Then set a pizza stone in the center of the smoker to preheat.

2. In a large zip-top bag, mix together the olive oil, garlic, cilantro, salt, and pepper. Add the shrimp and make sure they are completely coated in the mixture. Refrigerate for 30 minutes.

3. Place a perforated BBQ skillet on the grate of the smoker and let it preheat.

4. If you have a pizza pan, spread the dough onto it. If you only have a pizza peel, sprinkle it with cornmeal and then place the stretched dough on it. Ladle the alfredo sauce on it. Place the shrimp on the sauce. Sprinkle the red pepper flakes,

followed by the mozzarella and the Parmesan cheese, over the shrimp.

5. Carefully slide the pizza off the peel or pan and onto a pizza stone. Smoke the pizza for 15 to 20 minutes, until the crust is crisp and the sauce is bubbling.

6. Serve immediately.

KNOW YOUR INGREDIENTS: You could use crawfish instead of shrimp or add some hot sauce to the Alfredo sauce.

Smoked Shrimp with Spicy Peanut Sauce

SERVES 4

PREP TIME:
40 minutes

SMOKING TIME:
25 minutes

TEMPERATURE:
275°F

WOOD:
Alder or apple

This recipe is inspired by Southeast Asian cuisine, particularly that of Thailand. Serve this over rice noodles or jasmine rice for a delicious meal that you can have on the table in just over an hour, start to finish.

½ cup sesame oil, divided

¼ cup soy sauce

1 tablespoon minced garlic

1 teaspoon ground ginger

1 teaspoon freshly ground black pepper

24 jumbo shrimp (about 1½ pounds), peeled and deveined, tails left on

1 cup Spicy Peanut Sauce (page 174)

1. In a bowl, mix ¼ cup sesame oil, the soy sauce, garlic, ginger, and black pepper. Add the shrimp to the marinade and toss to coat completely. Cover the bowl and refrigerate for 30 minutes.

2. Preheat the smoker to 275°F. If using wooden skewers, soak them in water for at least 30 minutes.

3. To thread the shrimp onto skewers, hold the shrimp horizontally and run the skewer through one side, just below the head end, and out through the other side, just above the tail. Thread 4 shrimp onto each skewer.

4. In a saucepan on the stovetop, warm the peanut sauce over low heat.

5. Smoke the skewers for 10 minutes.

6. Baste the shrimp with the remaining ¼ cup sesame oil and smoke for another 5 minutes.

7. Remove the skewers and baste with the spicy peanut sauce. Return them to the smoker and smoke for 10 more minutes.

8. Serve warm.

SMOKING TIP: Use double skewers so the shrimp don't twirl. They're easier to turn and handle that way.

KNOW YOUR INGREDIENTS: If you'd like the shrimp to be spicier, add 1 teaspoon of cayenne pepper to the marinade. Additionally, you can substitute large shrimp for jumbo, which will take less time to smoke.

Smoked Oysters

SERVES 2

PREP TIME:
30 minutes

SMOKING TIME:
20 to
30 minutes

TEMPERATURE:
250°F

WOOD:
Alder or apple

There's no comparing freshly smoked oysters to the canned version. In this recipe, inspired by my family in Prince Edward Island, the umami of the ocean combines with the smoke and bacon, making this a full meal in and of itself.

2 slices smoked bacon

4 tablespoons (½ stick) unsalted butter, at room temperature

1 teaspoon minced garlic

½ teaspoon salt

½ teaspoon freshly ground black pepper

24 fresh oysters in the shell

1. In a skillet on the stovetop over medium heat, fry the bacon until it's crisp. When cool enough to handle, crumble it into small pieces.

2. In a small bowl, combine the butter, garlic, salt, and pepper. Stir in the bacon bits. Set aside in the refrigerator until ready to smoke.

3. Preheat the smoker to 250°F.

4. Shuck the oysters. Get rid of the top shells and leave the oysters in the bottom shells.

5. Arrange the oysters on a grill mat or grill screen. Add ½ teaspoon of the garlic-bacon butter to the top of each oyster.

6. Transfer the grill mat or screen to the smoker and smoke the oysters for 20 to 30 minutes, or until the edges of the oysters are curled and the internal temperature reaches 145°F.

7. Take the oysters out of the smoker, being careful not to spill the butter and juices. Let the oysters rest for 5 minutes before serving.

SMOKING TIP: You don't want to overcook the oysters, so watch them carefully for the last 10 minutes.

Smoked Whole Red Snapper

SERVES 4

PREP TIME:
20 minutes

SMOKING TIME:
3 hours
20 minutes

TEMPERATURE:
160°F
and 225°F

WOOD:
Apple, maple,
or peach

Red snapper has a light, firm, flaky texture and a mild taste. It takes well to smoking. For the best results, make sure you get it fresh, not frozen.

2 tablespoons unsalted butter, at room temperature

3 tablespoons olive oil, divided

2 teaspoons Fish Rub (page 167)

1 teaspoon minced garlic

½ teaspoon dried tarragon

1 (4- to 5-pound) whole red snapper, gutted and cleaned

5 lime slices (¼ inch thick)

1 scallion, coarsely chopped

1. Preheat the smoker to 160°F.

2. In a bowl, combine the butter, 2 tablespoons olive oil, the fish rub, garlic, and tarragon and mix them well. Rub the mixture all over the fish, including the inside. Place the lime slices and the chopped scallions in the belly cavity.

3. Coat a smoker rack with the remaining 1 tablespoon olive oil. Place the fish on a wire rack and set it in the smoker. (Or in a pellet smoker, just put the fish on the grates.) Smoke the fish for 1 hour.

4. Increase the smoker temperature to 225°F. Smoke the fish for another 2 hours to 2 hours 20 minutes, or until the internal temperature reaches 145°F.

5. Transfer the fish to a cutting board and let it rest for 5 minutes. Then you can fillet it or serve it in pieces.

SMOKING TIP: If you want the fish flakier, wait until the internal temperature is 165°F.

KNOW YOUR INGREDIENTS: Adding 1 teaspoon of cayenne pepper or red pepper flakes to the rub livens up the flavor.

Smoked Grouper

SERVES 4

PREP TIME:
40 minutes

SMOKING TIME:
30 minutes

TEMPERATURE:
225°F

WOOD:
Alder or apple

Buttery and firm, grouper has a mild flavor that's a touch sweet. With a texture between bass and halibut, it's a great fish to smoke. But it's pricey, so save this meal for a very special occasion.

1 tablespoon coarse salt

1 teaspoon freshly ground
  black pepper

1 teaspoon light brown sugar

1 (1-pound) grouper fillet

2 teaspoons olive oil

1 tablespoon Fish Rub (page 167)

1. In a bowl, mix together the salt, pepper, and brown sugar. Rub it into both sides of the fillet, then wrap the fillet in plastic and refrigerate for 30 minutes.

2. Preheat the smoker to 225°F.

3. Rub off the remaining brine from the fillet with paper towels. Brush both sides of the fish with the olive oil, then sprinkle with the fish rub.

4. Smoke the fillet for 30 minutes, or until the internal temperature reaches 145°F.

5. Let the fish rest for 5 minutes before serving.

SMOKING TIP: Don't dry-brine the grouper for more than 30 minutes. If you want the taste of the grouper to be sweeter, don't rub off the dry brine. Just pat the fillet dry with a paper towel and omit the olive oil and fish rub.

Smoked Lobster

SERVES 4

PREP TIME:
20 minutes

SMOKING TIME:
30 minutes

TEMPERATURE:
225°F

WOOD:
Apple
or cherry

Smoked lobster has a satisfying chew unlike any other smoked fish or meat. Talk about a decadent meal!

8 (5-ounce) lobster tails

8 tablespoons (1 stick) unsalted butter

2 tablespoons minced garlic

2 teaspoons salt

1 teaspoon freshly ground black pepper

1 teaspoon dried oregano

1 lemon, cut into wedges

1. If the lobster tails are frozen, slowly thaw them out in the refrigerator (this may take a whole day). Then remove them from the refrigerator and let them come almost to room temperature.

2. In a saucepan on the stovetop, melt the butter over low heat. Add the garlic, salt, pepper, and oregano and simmer for 2 minutes. Remove from the heat and set aside.

3. Preheat the smoker to 225°F. If using wooden skewers, soak them in water for at least 30 minutes.

4. Using kitchen scissors, cut through the lobster shell along the back, starting near the top, where the head used to be, to just before the fin. Then gently open the lobster tail, just a little, to expose the meat. Be careful not to break the back of the shell.

5. Push a skewer through the center of each lobster, from the head end toward the tail. It should poke out below the fin. This keeps the lobster tail from curling up.

6. Brush the meat side of the tails with the butter mixture. Place the lobsters shell-side down in the smoker and smoke for 30 minutes, or the internal temperature reaches 135°F. Baste with the butter mixture every 10 minutes.

7. Serve immediately with the lemon wedges.

Smoked Seafood Salad

SERVES 6

PREP TIME:
30 minutes

SMOKING TIME:
25 minutes

TEMPERATURE:
275°F

WOOD:
Apple
or cherry

Make any lunch a special occasion with this salad.

¾ cup olive oil, divided

4 tablespoons fresh
lime juice, divided

2 tablespoons Seafood
Seasoning (page 168)

2 tablespoons minced garlic

1 pound jumbo shrimp,
peeled and deveined

2 tablespoons honey

1 teaspoon grated lime zest

½ teaspoon salt

½ teaspoon freshly
ground black pepper

24 ounces salad greens,
such as mesclun

2 Smoked Lobster tails
(page 107), cut into
bite-size pieces

1. In a bowl, mix together ½ cup olive oil, 2 tablespoons lime juice, the seafood seasoning, and garlic. Add the shrimp to the marinade and coat them completely. Refrigerate for 30 minutes.

2. Preheat the smoker to 275°F. If using wooden skewers, soak them in water for at least 30 minutes.

3. To thread the shrimp onto skewers, hold the shrimp horizontally and run the skewer through one side, just below the head end, and out through the other side, just above the tail. Thread 4 shrimp onto each skewer. Reserve the marinade.

4. Smoke the shrimp for 10 minutes.

5. Baste the shrimp with the marinade, then return to the smoker for another 15 minutes. Take them out and let them rest for 10 minutes, then chop into bite-size pieces.

6. In a medium bowl, whisk together the remaining ¼ cup olive oil, 2 tablespoons lime juice, the honey, lime zest, salt, and pepper.

7. Place the salad greens in a large serving bowl. Scatter the shrimp and lobster over the leaves. Whisk the dressing again, pour it over the greens, and serve.

Smoked Crab Legs

SERVES 4

PREP TIME:
5 minutes

SMOKING TIME:
25 minutes

TEMPERATURE:
275°F

WOOD:
Alder, apple,
or cherry

A stack of these king crab legs is an actual feast. A little smoke really adds to the flavor of this seafood delicacy. They don't take a lot of time, so be careful not to overcook them. And don't be afraid to get crackin'!

10 pounds king crab legs

2 cups (4 sticks) unsalted butter

1 tablespoon minced garlic

1 tablespoon Seafood
Seasoning (page 168)

2 tablespoons chopped
fresh cilantro

2 or 3 lemons or limes,
cut into wedges

1. If the crab legs were frozen, thaw them completely in the refrigerator.

2. Preheat the smoker to 275°F.

3. In a saucepan on the stovetop, melt the butter over low heat. Add the garlic just as the butter melts, then stir in the seafood seasoning and cilantro and simmer for 90 seconds.

4. Brush the crab legs with the seasoned butter. Smoke them for 25 minutes, brushing them with the seasoned butter twice throughout and once again when you remove them.

5. Serve immediately with lemon wedges and the remaining seasoned butter for dipping.

SMOKING TIP: You might also try maple wood in this recipe. It's a good alternative to those listed because it also has a light smoke taste that doesn't take away from the unique and sweet taste of the crabmeat. After all, you paid a lot to get those king crab legs to the table!

SERVING TIP: This is enough crab for four people to have a huge meal of nothing but crab legs. However, if you are planning on serving other dishes at the meal, drop the total amount of crab to 6 pounds, which is 1½ pounds per person.

Smoked Mussels with Garlic Butter

SERVES 2

PREP TIME:
25 minutes

SMOKING TIME:
20 minutes

TEMPERATURE:
275°F

WOOD:
Maple or oak

You can get mussels all over the world and they're usually steamed, sometimes grilled. But with the light taste of smoke and a slathering of garlic butter, they're in a class of their own. And you can have them on the table in less than an hour!

2 pounds frozen mussels
in the shell

8 tablespoons (1 stick)
unsalted butter

1 tablespoon minced garlic

1 teaspoon dried oregano

1 teaspoon salt

1 teaspoon freshly ground
black pepper

1. Thaw the mussels in the fridge or in a plastic bag in a big bowl of water.

2. Preheat the smoker to 275°F.

3. Remove the top shell, leaving the mussel in the bottom shell. Arrange the mussels on wire racks or grill mats.

4. Transfer the mussel-topped wire rack or mat to the smoker and smoke for 10 minutes.

5. Meanwhile, in a saucepan on the stovetop, melt the butter over low heat. Add the garlic, oregano, salt, and pepper and simmer for 5 minutes over medium heat.

6. Spoon the butter mixture onto the mussels and smoke for another 10 minutes, so that they baste in their shells.

7. Remove the mussels from the smoker and serve immediately.

SMOKING TIP: Since the mussels take little time, you can use hickory wood to get a smokier flavor.

KNOW YOUR INGREDIENTS: You can try dried tarragon or dill instead of the oregano.

Smoked Halibut

SERVES 4

PREP TIME:
4 hours
30 minutes

SMOKING TIME:
2 hours

TEMPERATURE:
225°F

WOOD:
Alder, apple,
or maple

Halibut comes from Arctic waters. It's a huge flatfish, like flounder but 100 times bigger. The flesh has big flakes and a mild taste. This is an easy dish to make, and it goes great with some melted butter and a wedge of lemon.

1 tablespoon coarse salt

1 tablespoon granulated garlic

2 teaspoons freshly ground black pepper

2 (1-pound) skin-on halibut fillets

2 teaspoons olive oil

2 tablespoons Fish Rub (page 167)

1. In a small bowl, mix together the salt, granulated garlic, and pepper. Rub the mixture into the flesh side of the fillets. Tightly wrap each fillet in plastic and refrigerate for 4 hours.

2. Preheat the smoker to 225°F.

3. Pat the fish dry with paper towels. Brush both sides of the fillets with the olive oil. Generously sprinkle the fish rub on the flesh side. Let it come to room temperature for about 15 minutes.

4. Set the fillets skin-side down in the smoker and smoke for about 2 hours, or until the internal temperature reaches 145°F. Serve immediately.

SMOKING TIP: You can also smoke halibut steaks, but you'll need a grill screen or a nonstick perforated skillet. It will take less time, so keep an eye on the internal temperature. Because this is a lean fish, it's easy to overcook.

KNOW YOUR INGREDIENTS: I recommend using skin-on fillets because they are easier to smoke.

Smoked Salmon Pasta with Lemon and Dill

SERVES 4

PREP TIME:
3 hours
20 minutes

SMOKING TIME:
40 minutes

TEMPERATURE:
225°F

WOOD:
Apple, maple,
or peach

Lots of recipes for salmon pasta call for packaged smoked salmon. But when you hot-smoke it yourself, you'll never go back to the refrigerated section again.

FOR THE SALMON

1 (1-pound) skin-on salmon fillet

2 tablespoons coarse salt

2 tablespoons chopped
   fresh dill

1 tablespoon light brown sugar

2 teaspoons grated lemon zest

1 teaspoon freshly ground
   black pepper

FOR THE PASTA AND SAUCE

1 pound fettuccine or linguine

4 tablespoons (½ stick)
   unsalted butter

1 teaspoon minced garlic

1 teaspoon paprika

6 tablespoons white wine

2 cups heavy (whipping) cream

1 tablespoon chopped fresh dill

TO MAKE THE SALMON

1. Preheat the smoker to 225°F.

2. With needle-nose pliers or fish tweezers, remove any pin bones from the fillet.

3. In a bowl, mix together the salt, dill, brown sugar, lemon zest, and pepper. Rub the mixture into the flesh side of the salmon. Wrap the fillet tightly in plastic and refrigerate for 3 hours.

4. Unwrap the salmon and pat it dry with paper towels.

5. Smoke the salmon for 40 minutes, or until the internal temperature reaches 145°F.

6. Let the salmon rest while you prepare the pasta and sauce.

7. Cook the pasta according to the package directions.

8. In a large saucepan on the stovetop, melt the butter over medium-high heat. Add the garlic and sauté for 1 minute. Stir in the paprika and then the wine. Cook for 5 minutes to reduce, then add the cream. Cook over low heat, stirring occasionally, for about 7 minutes, or until the sauce gets a little thicker.

9. Meanwhile, cut the salmon into chunks.

10. When the sauce has reduced, stir the salmon in very gently.

11. Serve the salmon sauce over the pasta and sprinkle the chopped dill over the top.

SMOKING TIP: If you want a deeper color and taste of smoke, use a mix of cherry and hickory.

KNOW YOUR INGREDIENTS: You can use 1 tablespoon of maple syrup or maple sugar instead of brown sugar to cure the salmon.

Smoked Ahi Tuna with Sesame and Wasabi

SERVES 4

PREP TIME:
2 hours

SMOKING TIME:
1 hour

TEMPERATURE:
200°F

WOOD:
Alder, apple,
or peach

With this recipe, the tuna will be firm and have a light smoky taste that can't be matched on a grill. The wasabi sauce is good for tuna sandwiches, too.

FOR THE SMOKED TUNA

2 tablespoons coarse salt

1 tablespoon light brown sugar

1 teaspoon freshly ground black pepper

4 (6-ounce) ahi tuna steaks

2 tablespoons olive oil

¼ cup Seafood Seasoning (page 168)

1 tablespoon toasted sesame seeds, for serving

FOR THE WASABI SAUCE

¾ cup mayonnaise

1 tablespoon fresh lime juice

1 teaspoon sesame oil

2 teaspoons minced garlic

1 teaspoon wasabi powder or paste

TO SMOKE THE TUNA

1. In a small bowl, mix together the salt, brown sugar, and pepper. Rub the mixture into the tuna. Wrap the steaks in plastic and refrigerate for 2 hours.

2. Preheat the smoker to 200°F.

3. Wipe the dry brine off the tuna. Brush the tuna with the olive oil, then sprinkle the seafood seasoning on both sides of the steaks.

4. Smoke the tuna for about 1 hour, or until the internal temperature reaches 125°F for medium-rare or 140°F for medium.

5. Meanwhile, in a bowl, blend together the mayonnaise, lime juice, sesame oil, garlic, and wasabi. Refrigerate the sauce until serving time.

6. When the tuna steaks are done, lightly sprinkle them with the sesame seeds. Let them rest for 5 minutes, then serve them with the wasabi sauce on the side.

SMOKING TIP: If you are not using sushi-quality tuna, I recommend cooking it until the internal temperature reaches 140°F to be safe.

KNOW YOUR INGREDIENTS: If you want your tuna spicier, add 1 teaspoon of cayenne pepper to the dry brine.

Smoked Sea Bass

SERVES 4

PREP TIME:
3 hours
45 minutes

SMOKING TIME:
1 hour
45 minutes

TEMPERATURE:
200°F

WOOD:
Alder or apple

Striped bass are good to brine before smoking because they are not so oily. The fillets have a buttery taste and when you smoke them, the flesh is flaky. You don't have to season them too much to enjoy their sweet taste.

2 cups water

½ cup coarse salt

¼ cup packed light brown sugar

3 cups ice

½ cup white wine

1 tablespoon fresh lime juice

1 tablespoon minced garlic

1 tablespoon coarsely ground black pepper

2 (1-pound) skin-on striped bass fillets

¼ cup olive oil

2 teaspoons smoked paprika

1. In medium pot, bring the water almost to a boil. Add the salt and brown sugar and stir until the salt and sugar are dissolved. Remove from the heat and cool the brine down by adding the ice. Add the wine, lime juice, garlic, and pepper to the brine. Refrigerate the pot of brine until it is cold.

2. Use fish tweezers or needle-nose pliers to remove any bones from the bass fillets.

3. Place the fillets in a 2-gallon zip-top bag and pour the brine over them. Put the bag in a bowl (in case of leaks) and refrigerate for 3 hours.

4. Remove the fish from the brine and pat dry with paper towels. Brush both sides of the fillets with the olive oil, then sprinkle with the smoked paprika.

5. Let the fillets come up to room temperature for about 30 minutes.

6. Preheat the smoker to 200°F.

7. Smoke the fillets for 1 hour 45 minutes, or until the internal temperature reaches 140°F. Check after 1 hour 15 minutes to be safe and avoid overcooking.

8. Let the fillets rest for 5 minutes before serving.

KNOW YOUR INGREDIENTS: To make the sea bass richer and spicier, melt 4 tablespoons of butter with 1 teaspoon of Fish Rub (page 167) and a pinch of cayenne pepper. Spoon the mixture over the fillets before serving.

Smoked
Mac 'n' Cheese,
page 120

Chapter 6

Vegetables and Sides

SMOKED MEAT IS GREAT, BUT you should never forget the smoked side dishes. I have a few sides and vegetable dishes that you may not have thought of smoking before. Some of these recipes, like Smoked Cherry Tomatoes (page 142), can elevate ordinary salads and salsas. Others, like Smoked Mac 'n' Cheese (page 120) and Sicilian-Style Smoked Eggplant Salad (page 138), are excellent accompaniments to all your meaty mains. Be sure to check out the Smoky Creamed Spinach (page 128), which is perfect with a thick rib eye, and the Bacon-Wrapped Asparagus (page 124), which is so satisfying and delicious it could be a main course all on its own. Whatever types of veggies you're in the mood for, you'll find them here. And pro tip: Once you smoke veggies with a balsamic reduction, you may never cook them another way.

Smoked Mac 'n' Cheese

SERVES 6 TO 8

PREP TIME:
20 minutes

SMOKING TIME:
50 minutes

TEMPERATURE:
225°F

WOOD:
Hickory

Mac 'n' cheese is a real all-American dish. This recipe is creamy, bubbly, melty, and crunchy on top. Its wonderful smoky flavor makes it perfect to pair with any type of BBQ.

FOR THE MAC 'N' CHEESE

4 tablespoons (½ stick) unsalted butter

¼ cup all-purpose flour

3 cups whole milk

8 ounces cream cheese, in chunks

1 teaspoon salt

½ teaspoon freshly ground black pepper

½ cup shredded sharp cheddar cheese

½ cup shredded Gouda cheese

¼ cup shredded Parmesan cheese

1 pound elbow macaroni, cooked according to package directions

FOR THE TOPPING

2 cups fine dried bread crumbs or panko

8 tablespoons (1 stick) unsalted butter, melted

1 teaspoon dried thyme

1 teaspoon dried rosemary

1 teaspoon poultry seasoning

TO MAKE THE MAC 'N' CHEESE

1. Preheat the smoker to 225°F.

2. In a large saucepan on the stovetop, melt the butter over low heat. Whisk in the flour, increase the heat to medium, and cook for 2 minutes. Whisk in the milk and bring to a boil, then remove from the heat.

3. Stir in the cream cheese, salt, and pepper until smooth. Mix in the cheddar, Gouda, and Parmesan.

4. Spread the cooked macaroni in a 9½-by-11-by-2-inch roasting pan. Pour the cheese sauce over the macaroni, then gently fold it together until all the pasta is well coated.

TO MAKE THE TOPPING

5. In a large bowl, combine the bread crumbs, melted butter, thyme, rosemary, and poultry seasoning. Sprinkle the bread crumb mixture over the pasta.

6. Smoke the mac 'n' cheese for 50 minutes.

7. Serve warm.

COOKING TIP: Let the pasta cool for 10 minutes before adding the cheese sauce.

KNOW YOUR INGREDIENTS: Try substituting 1 cup of Guinness stout for 1 cup of the milk in the cheese sauce. If you're looking for a fancier presentation, try adding some chopped hazelnuts on top of the mac before serving.

PAIR IT WITH: This pasta dish goes great with—or in—Pulled Pork Sandwiches (page 47).

Smoked Garlic Tzatziki Sauce

SERVES 8

PREP TIME:
1 hour
20 minutes

SMOKING TIME:
40 minutes

TEMPERATURE:
250°F

WOOD:
Maple or oak

Tzatziki, made with Greek yogurt and cucumber, is the perfect partner to marinated and grilled beef or pork. This is my friend Gus's recipe. Gus says that he has made it since he was 12 years old and learned from his grandfather, who was a chef on the cruise liners *Olympia* and *Anna Maria*. One day, we were playing around with ideas for how we could smoke tzatziki and figured out that smoking the garlic was the way to go.

1 large head garlic

3 tablespoons extra-virgin olive oil, divided

1 English cucumber, partially peeled (striped) and grated

2 teaspoons coarse salt, divided

1 cup 0% plain Greek yogurt

1 teaspoon distilled white vinegar

¼ teaspoon ground white pepper

1. Preheat the smoker to 250°F.

2. Cut the top off the garlic head, set it cut-side up, and drizzle with 1 tablespoon olive oil.

3. Set the garlic in the smoker on a piece of aluminum foil. Smoke the garlic for 40 minutes, or until soft and browned.

4. Let the garlic cool, then squeeze out half of the garlic cloves (save the remainder for another use).

5. In a colander set in the sink, toss the cucumber with 1 teaspoon salt and let stand for 15 to 20 minutes.

6. Pour the cucumber out onto a clean kitchen towel and squeeze out as much liquid as you can.

7. In a large bowl, stir together the yogurt, smoked garlic, vinegar, white pepper, 1 tablespoon olive oil, and the remaining 1 teaspoon salt.

8. Add the grated cucumber to the yogurt mixture and stir to combine. Cover tightly and refrigerate for 1 to 2 hours. The longer it rests, the more the garlic infuses it with smoky flavor.

9. When ready to serve, stir the tzatziki sauce, transfer to a serving bowl, and drizzle with the remaining 1 tablespoon olive oil.

KNOW YOUR INGREDIENTS: I use organic 0% Greek yogurt, but you can use 2% or whole-milk Greek yogurt.

PAIR IT WITH: Take a warm pita bread, pick up a piece of meat, add a dollop of tzatziki—that's the lunch of the gods. This sauce also goes great with a sliced or wedged ripe tomato topped with feta, a drizzle of olive oil, oregano, a sprinkle of salt, and a little fresh parsley.

Bacon-Wrapped Asparagus

SERVES 4

PREP TIME:
30 minutes

SMOKING TIME:
2 hours

TEMPERATURE:
275°F

WOOD:
Apple,
hickory,
or maple

Bacon makes everything better, including asparagus. I promise you: When the flavors of the smoke, bacon, and asparagus meld after a couple of hours, something magical happens.

12 slices bacon

1 teaspoon salt

1 teaspoon freshly ground
black pepper

1 teaspoon garlic powder

24 thin asparagus spears,
tough ends trimmed

1. Preheat the smoker to 275°F.

2. Lay the bacon on a wire rack or grill screen (or directly on the smoker rack, perpendicular to the grate) and smoke for 30 minutes.

3. Meanwhile, in a small bowl, mix together the salt, pepper, and garlic powder. Sprinkle it over the asparagus.

4. Take the partially cooked bacon out of the smoker (leave the smoker on).

5. Let the bacon cool for 5 minutes. Wrap 1 bacon slice around 2 spears of seasoned asparagus, starting at the bottom of the stalks. You can use a toothpick to make the bacon stay in place if needed.

6. Place the bacon-wrapped asparagus on the cooking rack and smoke for 1 hour 30 minutes, or until the bacon is nicely crisped (but not overly so).

7. Serve warm.

KNOW YOUR INGREDIENTS: I like spicy asparagus, so I always add 1 teaspoon of cayenne pepper to the seasoning.

Smoked Potatoes and Onions

SERVES 8

PREP TIME:
20 minutes

SMOKING TIME:
2 hours

TEMPERATURE:
250°F

WOOD:
Apple, cherry,
or hickory

The potatoes in this recipe are paired with sweet onions, spices, and smoke to make a great side for your main attraction. I highly recommend it as one of the staples on your holiday menu.

2 pounds baby red potatoes

2 large sweet onions, such as Vidalia or Walla Walla

6 tablespoons olive oil

1 tablespoon minced garlic

1 tablespoon ground rosemary

1 tablespoon coarse salt

1 tablespoon coarsely ground black pepper

2 tablespoons chopped fresh parsley

4 ounces Parmesan cheese, grated

1. Preheat the smoker to 250°F.

2. Scrub the potatoes and cut them in half. Pat them dry with paper towels.

3. Thinly slice the onions and place them on the bottom of a shallow baking dish. Place a layer of potatoes over the onions.

4. In a small bowl, mix together the olive oil, garlic, rosemary, salt, and pepper. Brush the potatoes with the seasoned oil.

5. Set the pan in the smoker and smoke for 2 hours, or until the potatoes are fork-tender.

6. Take the potatoes out of the smoker, sprinkle them with the parsley, and toss to combine everything. Let rest for 5 minutes.

7. Sprinkle the Parmesan over the pan. Toss again, transfer to a serving dish, and it's good to go.

SMOKING TIP: Use a nonstick perforated BBQ skillet and you'll get more of the smoky flavor into the onions.

Smoked Potato Salad with Bacon

SERVES 4

PREP TIME:
30 minutes

SMOKING TIME:
40 minutes

TEMPERATURE:
275°F

WOOD:
Cherry

There are a lot of ways to make potato salad. So why not make this your signature? Smoking the potatoes and the bacon adds a new, delicious touch to a familiar dish that could become your calling card.

FOR THE POTATO SALAD

1½ pounds red potatoes or other small potatoes

¼ cup olive oil

2 teaspoons garlic powder

1 teaspoon dried oregano

1 tablespoon coarse salt

1 teaspoon freshly ground black pepper

6 slices bacon

1 celery stalk, diced

1 cup finely chopped red onion

FOR THE DRESSING

1½ cups mayonnaise

2 tablespoons apple cider vinegar

2 tablespoons whole-grain mustard

1 tablespoon granulated sugar

1 teaspoon celery seed

1 teaspoon garlic powder

1 teaspoon paprika

1 teaspoon salt

1 teaspoon freshly ground black pepper

TO MAKE THE POTATO SALAD

1. Preheat the smoker to 275°F.

2. Scrub the potatoes under cold water and dry them with paper towels.

3. In a small bowl, mix together the olive oil, garlic powder, oregano, salt, and pepper. Brush the potatoes with some of the mixture.

4. Set the potatoes in the smoker. Arrange the bacon on a wire rack or grill screen and set on a rack above the potatoes. Smoke for 35 minutes, or until the bacon is crisp. Remove the bacon and chop into small pieces.

5. Brush the potatoes with the rest of the olive oil mixture and smoke for 5 more minutes, or until the potatoes are fork-tender and their internal temperature reaches 210°F.

6. Let the potatoes rest for 20 minutes.

7. Cut the potatoes into chunks and place them in a large bowl. Sprinkle the chopped bacon, celery, and onion over the potatoes.

TO MAKE THE DRESSING

8. In a small bowl, whisk together the mayonnaise, vinegar, mustard, sugar, celery seed, garlic powder, paprika, salt, and pepper.

9. Pour the dressing over the vegetables and stir to combine. Cover the bowl and refrigerate for 30 minutes before serving.

KNOW YOUR INGREDIENTS: I like my potatoes with the skin on and spicy, so I add a couple shots of hot sauce when mixing the dressing.

Smoky Creamed Spinach

SERVES 8

PREP TIME:
20 minutes

SMOKING TIME:
10 minutes

TEMPERATURE:
275°F

WOOD:
Apple, cherry,
or pecan

This version of creamed spinach uses a perforated BBQ skillet to let the smoke surround the spinach. With the rich cream and cheese sauce, this dish goes nicely with smoked turkey or beef.

1 pound spinach
  leaves, stemmed

¼ cup olive oil

1 teaspoon garlic powder

1 teaspoon salt

1 teaspoon freshly ground
  black pepper

6 tablespoons unsalted butter

1 teaspoon cayenne pepper

1 teaspoon grated nutmeg

1 cup heavy (whipping) cream

4 ounces cream cheese,
  cut into chunks

½ cup shredded Gouda cheese

1. Preheat the smoker to 275°F.

2. Rinse the spinach leaves and pat dry with paper towels. Set in a bowl.

3. In a small bowl, mix together the olive oil with the garlic powder, salt, and pepper. Add the seasoned oil to the spinach and toss to coat all the leaves.

4. Place the spinach in a perforated BBQ skillet (ideally non-stick) and smoke for 10 minutes. Remove and chop up.

5. In a large saucepan on the stovetop, heat the butter over medium heat. Stir in the cayenne and nutmeg. Pour in the heavy cream and cook, stirring, for about 7 minutes, or until it thickens. Add the cream cheese and stir until it's blended. Add the chopped spinach and Gouda and stir to combine.

6. Serve immediately.

KNOW YOUR INGREDIENTS: Bring it to another level and add 2 tablespoons or grated Romano and 2 tablespoons of grated Parmesan.

Smoked Vegetable Casserole

SERVES 6

PREP TIME:
10 minutes

SMOKING TIME:
1 hour
30 minutes

TEMPERATURE:
225°F

WOOD:
Apple, cherry,
or pecan

Caramelized summer vegetables, smoked low and slow, are unmatched, especially when their slightly sweet flavors are paired with balsamic vinegar.

1 zucchini, cut into
½-inch-thick slices

1 yellow summer squash, cut into ½-inch-thick slices

1 carrot, cut into ½-inch-thick slices

1 red onion, cut into eighths

1 green bell pepper, cut into eighths

1 red bell pepper, cut into eighths

1 yellow bell pepper, cut into eighths

¼ cup olive oil

2 tablespoons balsamic vinegar

1 tablespoon maple syrup

3 tablespoons minced garlic

2 teaspoons coarse salt

1 teaspoon freshly ground black pepper

1. Preheat the smoker to 225°F.

2. Place the zucchini, squash, carrot, onion, and bell peppers in a large bowl. In a small bowl, whisk together the olive oil, vinegar, maple syrup, garlic, salt, and black pepper. Add the dressing to the vegetables. Mix them up, making sure all the vegetables are coated.

3. Place them in a glass baking dish. Smoke for 1 hour 30 minutes, or until tender and caramelized.

4. Serve immediately.

SMOKING TIPS: You can also smoke the vegetables in a nonstick perforated BBQ skillet or grill basket. If you have a pellet grill, preheat it to 350°F. The vegetables should be ready in 40 minutes.

KNOW YOUR INGREDIENTS: Besides the vegetables listed, you can also add pieces of corn on the cob or sliced beets. Try honey or 1 tablespoon of molasses mixed with 1 teaspoon of brown sugar instead of the maple syrup.

Smoked Tofu and Vegetables

SERVES 4

PREP TIME:
2 hours
15 minutes

SMOKING TIME:
1 hour
30 minutes

TEMPERATURE:
225°F

WOOD:
Beechnut,
hickory,
or pecan

When tofu is marinated and smoked low and slow, the texture gets denser and the seasonings concentrate. It only gets better when you add crunchy snow peas and baby corn.

1 (16-ounce) block firm or extra-firm tofu

½ cup soy sauce

½ cup sesame oil

4 scallions, chopped

2 tablespoons minced garlic

1 teaspoon ground ginger

8 ounces baby corn, preferably fresh (but canned or frozen okay)

8 ounces snow peas

1 tablespoon salt

2 teaspoons freshly ground black pepper

1 teaspoon red pepper flakes

1 tablespoon sesame seeds

1. Set the block of tofu on a cutting board. Place another cutting board on top, then stack two dinner plates on it. Leave the tofu to press for 40 minutes, draining off the water as needed. Once pressed, cut the block into ½-inch-thick slices and place in a shallow baking dish.

2. In a small bowl, mix together the soy sauce, sesame oil, scallions, garlic, and ginger. Spoon half of the marinade over the tofu, coating all sides.

3. Arrange the baby corn and snow pea pods in a separate baking dish. Add the remaining marinade and toss to coat them.

4. Cover both baking dishes and refrigerate for 1 hour.

5. Take the dishes out of the fridge and let them sit on the counter, still covered, for about 30 minutes.

6. Preheat the smoker to 225°F and fill the water pan.

7. Arrange the tofu, baby corn, and snow peas on a grill screen. Sprinkle the vegetables with the salt, black pepper, and pepper flakes.

8. Set the grill racks in the smoker. Smoke for 1 hour 30 minutes.

9. Cut the tofu slices into chunks and put in a serving bowl. Scatter the baby corn and snow peas over the tofu. Sprinkle the sesame seeds on top. Gently mix and serve immediately.

PAIR IT WITH: This dish goes great with any of the chicken, pork, and shrimp recipes in this cookbook that are inspired by East and Southeast Asian flavor profiles, such as Smoked Javanese-Style Chicken Satay with Spicy Peanut Sauce (page 32) or Korean-Style Short Ribs (page 80). Otherwise, it can be the main dish for a meatless meal.

Smoked Creamed Corn

SERVES 8

PREP TIME:
30 minutes

SMOKING TIME:
45 minutes

TEMPERATURE:
275°F

WOOD:
Apple, cherry,
or pecan

This Southwest-inspired version of creamed corn works well for a big holiday celebration. Try pairing it with a smoked turkey, pork, or brisket.

8 ears corn, husked

¼ cup olive oil

1 teaspoon salt

1 teaspoon freshly ground
  black pepper

1 teaspoon garlic powder

4 slices bacon

6 tablespoons unsalted butter

2 teaspoons light brown sugar

1 teaspoon ancho powder

1 teaspoon chipotle powder

1 teaspoon grated nutmeg

1 cup heavy (whipping) cream

½ cup shredded
  Gruyère cheese

1. Preheat the smoker to 275°F.

2. Remove any silk from the corn. Brush the ears with the olive oil, then sprinkle with the salt, pepper, and garlic powder.

3. Place the corn in the smoker. Arrange the bacon slices on a wire rack or grill screen (or directly on the smoker rack, perpendicular to the grate). Smoke for 45 minutes, or until the ears have turned brown and the bacon is cooked.

4. Slice the kernels off the ears into a bowl. Crumble the bacon and add it to the bowl.

5. In a large saucepan on the stovetop, melt the butter over medium heat. Stir in the brown sugar, ancho chili powder, chipotle powder, and nutmeg. Add the heavy cream and stir the mixture until it slightly thickens.

6. Mix in the smoked corn and bacon and let it simmer for 5 minutes.

7. Stir in the Gruyère and serve immediately.

Smoked Corn on the Cob

SERVES 4

PREP TIME:
1 hour

SMOKING TIME:
1 hour

TEMPERATURE:
250°F

WOOD:
Apple, maple,
or hickory

In July and August, corn is at its peak. To accompany any smoked or grilled food, there's nothing that reminds me more of summer than corn. Soaking the corn will make the kernels absorb a little water. Then the juicy corn is infused with steam, spices, and smoke—can't ya just taste it?

8 large ears corn, husked

½ cup olive oil

1 tablespoon garlic powder

1 tablespoon smoked salt

2 teaspoons freshly ground black pepper

1. Remove any silk from the corn and soak the ears in cold water for 1 hour. Do not add salt to the water because it makes the kernels shrink.

2. Preheat the smoker to 250°F.

3. In a small bowl, mix together the olive oil, garlic powder, smoked salt, and pepper. Pull the corn out of the water, pat the ears dry with paper towels, and brush them with the seasoned olive oil.

4. Smoke the corn for 1 hour, or until the kernels are tender and slightly browned. Brush the corn with the olive oil mix every 20 minutes.

5. Serve hot.

KNOW YOUR INGREDIENTS: If you want a real cowboy version of smoked corn, use mesquite wood, add red pepper flakes to the oil, and increase the temperature to 275° F. Check to see if it's done after about 45 minutes.

Smoked Corn Salsa

SERVES 6

PREP TIME:
25 minutes

SMOKING TIME:
35 minutes

TEMPERATURE:
275°F

WOOD:
Apple
or cherry

This Mexican-inspired recipe goes well with chicken, fish, pork, and beef. It always tastes like summertime to me. When you see cherries and corn in Canada, that's when you know it's summer. When I used to do the trade shows, there was different corn everywhere. There was sweet corn out west in Alberta, and colored varieties in the eastern provinces. Corn holds a special place in my smoky heart.

6 ears corn, husked

4 tablespoons olive oil, divided

2 tablespoons garlic powder

1 tablespoon salt

1 tablespoon freshly
  ground black pepper

1 tablespoon minced garlic

12 large mushrooms, sliced

1 teaspoon fresh thyme, or dried

Juice of 1 lime

1. Preheat the smoker to 275°F.

2. Remove any silk from the corn. Brush the corn with 2 tablespoons olive oil. In a small bowl, mix together the garlic powder, salt, and pepper. Sprinkle the mixture over the corn.

3. Smoke the corn for 35 minutes, or until slightly browned and tender.

4. Let the corn cool for about 10 minutes.

5. In a large skillet on the stovetop, heat the remaining 2 tablespoons olive oil and the minced garlic over medium heat. Add the mushrooms and sauté for 4 minutes. Stir in the thyme and sauté for 1 more minute, or until the mushrooms are soft and juicy.

6. Cut the kernels off the cobs (I recommend using a knife with a serrated edge) into a bowl. Add the mushrooms and their juices. Pour the lime juice over the ingredients and mix it all up.

7. Serve immediately or cover and refrigerate to serve chilled.

KNOW YOUR INGREDIENTS: It's not a bad idea to chop up some roasted red peppers and add them to the corn and mushrooms. If you want more of an authentic Mexican flavor, add a chopped habanero pepper or 2 teaspoons of red pepper flakes and refrigerate for 1 hour to let the spices blend in.

Smoked and Stuffed Zucchini

SERVES 4

PREP TIME:
15 minutes

SMOKING TIME:
1 hour

TEMPERATURE:
225°F

WOOD:
Hickory
or maple

This is a hearty side dish that could easily be a main course on its own. The zucchini halves and cheese take on a smoky taste that goes great with almost every main course.

4 medium zucchini

5 teaspoons olive oil

1 tablespoon salt

2 teaspoons freshly ground black pepper

2 teaspoons garlic powder

2 teaspoons paprika

1 small red onion, finely chopped

½ cup seasoned croutons

½ cup shredded mozzarella cheese

3 tablespoons grated Parmesan cheese

1. Preheat the smoker to 225°F.

2. Wash the zucchini. Halve the zucchini lengthwise, then slice off a thin strip down the length of each half to allow the zucchini to lie flat.

3. With a teaspoon or melon baller, scoop out the pulp and seeds to make 8 zucchini boats, leaving about ⅛ inch of wall all around. Pat the outside of the zucchini dry with paper towels.

4. In a small bowl, mix together the oil, salt, pepper, garlic powder, and paprika. Brush the inside and outside of the zucchini boats with about 2 teaspoons of the seasoned oil.

5. In a skillet on the stovetop, heat the remaining seasoned oil over medium-high heat. Add the onion and sauté for about 3 minutes, or until softened. Remove from the heat and stir in the croutons.

6. Spoon the mixture into the zucchini boats.

7. Place the zucchini boats on a cooking rack or grill grate in the smoker. Smoke for 45 minutes.

8. Sprinkle the boats with the mozzarella and Parmesan. Return to the smoker for another 15 minutes.

9. Serve immediately.

KNOW YOUR INGREDIENTS: Sometimes I like to use smoked salt and smoked paprika for this recipe. To make the zucchini boats even more substantial, use cooked sausage and bread crumbs instead of the croutons.

Sicilian-Style Smoked Eggplant Salad

SERVES 4

PREP TIME:
30 minutes

SMOKING TIME:
45 minutes

TEMPERATURE:
225°F

WOOD:
Apple or oak

This Sicilian-inspired smoked eggplant bursts with the tastes of summer: smoke and fire. Sitting in the backyard with my friend Vinny, both in Toronto and Florida, we would enjoy this as a starter, or antipasto, with smoked sausage while he was grilling big steaks, Tuscan style.

2 large eggplants

½ cup olive oil, plus
  2 tablespoons

¼ cup balsamic vinegar

4 teaspoons coarse salt

1 tablespoon granulated garlic

2 teaspoons red pepper flakes

1 teaspoon dried oregano

1 small red onion, diced

1 tablespoon minced garlic

1 red bell pepper, diced

2 plum tomatoes, diced

2 bay leaves

½ cup diced Sicilian olives

1 tablespoon chopped
  fresh basil

2 tablespoons pine nuts

1. Preheat the smoker to 225°F.

2. Cut the eggplant into 1-inch cubes and place them in a large bowl.

3. In a medium bowl, mix together ½ cup olive oil, the vinegar, salt, granulated garlic, red pepper flakes, and oregano. Pour the oil mixture over the cubed eggplant and toss to coat. Cover the bowl and let it rest for 15 minutes.

4. Arrange the eggplant cubes on a grill screen and set them in the smoker. Smoke for 45 minutes.

5. About 20 minutes before the eggplant is done, in a large skillet on the stovetop, heat the remaining 2 tablespoons oil over medium-high heat. Add the onion and cook for 2 minutes. Add the minced garlic and bell pepper and sauté for another 3 minutes. Add the tomatoes and bay leaves and cook for another 15 minutes, stirring every few minutes, until the liquid is mostly reduced, just a little saucy.

6. Remove the eggplant from the smoker and transfer it to a large bowl. Sprinkle in the olives, basil, and pine nuts.

7. Discard the bay leaves and spoon the onion/pepper/tomato mixture over the eggplant. Mix it together gently.

8. Serve the salad hot or keep it covered and serve warm.

KNOW YOUR INGREDIENTS: Sprinkle the salad with grated Parmesan cheese or crumbled goat cheese before serving, if desired. Additionally, using balsamic reduction instead of the vinegar gives the eggplant a slightly caramelized taste.

Smoked Stuffed Artichokes

SERVES 4

PREP TIME:
1 hour

SMOKING TIME:
1 hour
30 minutes

TEMPERATURE:
275°F

WOOD:
Alder, cherry,
or pecan

These smoked artichokes are super fun to eat because you pull off the leaves one by one and scrape the delicious meat off with your teeth. They're a great unexpected starter or side dish. Serve them with wedges of lime for a burst of citrus.

4 large artichokes

4 teaspoons fresh lime juice, divided

4 slices smoked bacon

4 tablespoons (½ stick) unsalted butter

1 yellow onion, cut into medium dice

2 tablespoons minced garlic

¾ cup white wine

8 cups seasoned bread crumbs

1½ cups chopped fresh parsley

4 tablespoons grated Romano cheese

1. Preheat the smoker to 275°F.

2. Wash the artichokes with lots of cold water. Cut just enough off the bottom of each artichoke so that it sits flat. Remove the tough outer leaves. Use kitchen scissors to cut any of the pointy ends off the rest of the leaves. Pull the leaves in the middle open. With a spoon that has a sharp edge (like a grapefruit spoon), dig out the fuzzy choke in the center by scraping it away. Sprinkle the 2 teaspoons lime juice over the artichokes.

3. In a vegetable steamer, steam the artichokes for 15 minutes. Set them aside.

4. In a skillet on the stovetop, fry the bacon over high heat for about 5 minutes, or until crisp. Remove the bacon and drain on paper towels. Reduce the heat to medium. Add the butter and onion to the bacon fat and sauté for 2 minutes. Add the garlic and cook for another 5 minutes, or until the onion is tender and translucent. Stir in the wine and remaining 2 teaspoons lime juice and simmer, stirring, for another 5 minutes.

5. Mix in the seasoned bread crumbs and parsley. Remove the pan from the heat and let the mixture rest for about 10 minutes.

6. Set the steamed artichokes on the cooking rack. Fill the middle of the artichokes and in between the leaves with the seasoned bread crumb mixture. Spread the leaves out as you work to be able to fit all the stuffing.

7. Place the artichokes on the grill rack in the smoker. Smoke for 1 hour 10 minutes.

8. Remove the artichokes and sprinkle each with 1 tablespoon Romano. Return them to the smoker for 20 minutes.

9. Serve hot.

SMOKING TIP: For a pellet smoker, set it to 350°F and smoke the artichokes for 45 minutes, add the cheese, and smoke for another 10 minutes.

KNOW YOUR INGREDIENTS: You can sprinkle 2 teaspoons of cayenne pepper in the bread crumbs for a spicier dish.

Smoked Cherry Tomatoes

SERVES 4

PREP TIME:
15 minutes

SMOKING TIME:
1 hour

TEMPERATURE:
225°F

WOOD:
Apple, cherry,
or maple

They may be small, but these little red gems come out tangy with a twist of sweetness and the flavor of smoke. The heat concentrates their flavor so beautifully you'll want to eat them like candy. Bring the recipe up another level by sprinkling crumbled blue or feta cheese over the tomatoes before serving them.

2 pounds cherry
tomatoes, halved

¼ cup olive oil

1 tablespoon minced garlic

1 tablespoon coarse salt

2 teaspoons chipotle
powder (optional)

2 teaspoons dried basil

1 teaspoon freshly ground
black pepper

¼ cup balsamic reduction

1. Preheat the smoker to 225°F.

2. Arrange the tomatoes in a large, shallow baking dish.

3. In a small bowl, mix together the olive oil, garlic, salt, chipotle powder (if using), basil, and black pepper. Brush the mixture over the tomatoes.

4. Smoke the tomatoes for 30 minutes.

5. Sprinkle the balsamic reduction over the tomatoes and smoke for another 30 minutes.

6. Let the tomatoes rest for 10 minutes before serving.

KNOW YOUR INGREDIENTS: You can use grape tomatoes, but keep in mind they will be done a little sooner that the cherry tomatoes. You can also substitute beef, poultry, or seafood seasoning on the tomatoes, depending on the main course. These tomatoes are also delicious on the Smoked Seafood Pizza (page 100). Lastly, instead of balsamic reduction, you can use 1 tablespoon of brown sugar mixed with 3 tablespoons of molasses.

Smoked Whole Onions

PREP TIME:
15 minutes

SMOKING TIME:
1 hour
30 minutes

TEMPERATURE:
275°F

WOOD:
Apple, cherry,
or pecan

These smoked onions are so easy to make, and they go with every beef, pork, poultry, and fish recipe you can imagine. If you can't find Vidalia onions, Walla Walla sweet onions are a good substitute. In a pinch, go for large yellow onions.

4 large Vidalia onions

4 tablespoons (½ stick)
unsalted butter

4 teaspoons coarse salt

2 teaspoons freshly
ground black pepper

1 teaspoon garlic powder

1. Preheat the smoker to 275°F.

2. Slice the bottom of the onions, just above the root, so that they can sit flat. Then slice off the top of the onions.

3. With a paring knife, cut out a circle at the top of the onion that's about 1½ inches deep. Be sure that you don't cut through the bottom of the onion.

4. Wrap the bottom half of each onion with aluminum foil. Be sure that the onions are flat and not tilted.

5. Place 1 tablespoon butter on the top of each onion, then sprinkle with the salt, pepper, and garlic powder.

6. Smoke the onions for 1 hour 30 minutes. or until the skins have turned a golden-brown color.

7. Let the onions rest for 5 minutes before serving.

SMOKING TIP: If you would like a bigger smoke flavor, try hickory or even mesquite.

KNOW YOUR INGREDIENTS: Instead of the salt, pepper, and garlic, use 2 tablespoons of beef, poultry, or seafood rub, depending on what else you're smoking. Experiment by adding ½ teaspoon of brown sugar or maple syrup if you would like the onions to be caramelized.

Basque-Style
Cheesecake,
page 158

Chapter 7

Starters, Snacks, and Desserts

NOW THAT I'VE TAKEN YOU through the main courses and side dishes, let's talk about everything else, like starters, snacks, and desserts. You've seen smoked cheese and nuts in the stores, but did you know how easy it is to make them in your electric smoker? I'll show you how and then some. Thinking about brunch? Check out the Smoked Salmon Spread (page 146) or the Stuffed and Smoked French Toast (page 156). And if you want to start the party, be sure to check out the Smoked Spicy Queso Dip (page 148). For dessert, I turn up the heat. Check out the amazing foods you can bake in a pellet smoker, like the Basque-Style Cheesecake (page 158) or the Smoked Pineapple Chocolate Upside-Down Cake (page 160). Lastly, make sure you prepare multiple batches of the Smoked Candied Nuts (page 151). I promise you'll be craving them. They also make awesome gifts for the holidays!

Smoked Salmon Spread

SERVES 6

PREP TIME:
1 hour,
15 minutes
(see
Smoking tip)

Enjoy this fabulous smoked fish spread for a snack, as a starter, or in a sandwich. No matter how you eat it, you'll wish you'd made more.

8 ounces cream cheese, at room temperature

¼ cup heavy (whipping) cream

½ cup chopped scallions

1 tablespoon minced capers (optional)

2 teaspoons chopped fresh dill

1 teaspoon garlic powder

1 teaspoon freshly ground black pepper

8 ounces Canadian-Style Smoked Salmon on Cedar (page 99), finely chopped

In a large bowl, blend together the cream cheese and cream until smooth. Stir in the scallions, capers (if using), dill, garlic powder, and pepper. Add the salmon and stir to evenly distribute. Cover and refrigerate for 1 hour before serving.

SMOKING TIP: When you make the smoked salmon, just throw on an extra ½ pound of fish to have for this spread. Note that the smoking time, temperature, and wood listed here are all for the smoked salmon recipe. The prep time for the spread itself is 1 hour 15 minutes.

KNOW YOUR INGREDIENTS: For a spicier spread, add 1 teaspoon of cayenne pepper or horseradish.

Smoked Cheddar Cheese

SERVES 6

PREP TIME:
4 hours

SMOKING TIME:
1 hour

TEMPERATURE:
125°F

WOOD:
Hickory

What could be simpler than a smoked cheese appetizer? Make multiple blocks and keep them in the fridge. The smoky flavor gets deeper the longer you leave it.

3 (8-ounce) blocks aged
  cheddar cheese

1. Preheat the smoker to 125°F.

2. Set the blocks of cheese away from the hottest part of the smoker. Smoke them for 1 hour.

3. Let the cheese cool to room temperature, then put them in separate zip-top bags and refrigerate for at least 4 hours before serving.

PAIR IT WITH: This is a wonderful after-dinner treat with Smoked Almonds (page 150) or Smoked Candied Nuts (page 151).

KNOW YOUR INGREDIENTS: Sprinkle a little cayenne pepper over the cheese to liven it up when you serve it. Soft cheese melts at any temperature above this, but you can safely smoke Gouda, Monterey Jack, or Swiss this way.

Smoked Spicy Queso Dip

SERVES 4

PREP TIME:
15 minutes

COOK TIME:
2 hours

TEMPERATURE:
250°F

WOOD:
Hickory or
mesquite

This Tex-Mex-inspired smoked cheese dip is easy to make. Experiment with the woods to really get the most out of the smoke, cheese, and spices. Before long, you'll find the combo that makes you stand out in the wide world of queso dip.

2 tablespoons unsalted butter

1 medium red onion, diced

1 tablespoon minced garlic

1 jalapeño pepper,
  seeded and diced

1 pound Velveeta cheese,
  cut into 1-inch cubes

¾ cup drained canned
  diced tomatoes

1 teaspoon hot sauce

Chips, for dipping

1. Preheat the smoker to 250°F and fill the water pan.

2. In a skillet on the stovetop, heat the butter over medium heat. Add the onion and garlic and sauté for 5 to 7 minutes, until tender and translucent.

3. Transfer the sautéed onion and garlic to a shallow aluminum baking dish or 12-inch cast-iron skillet and add the jalapeño and Velveeta. Stir it all up to make sure everything is mixed.

4. Smoke the cheese mixture for 2 hours. As soon as the cheese starts to melt, stir in the diced tomatoes and hot sauce. After that, stir the queso every 30 minutes.

5. Remove the pan from the smoker and stir the dip a final time until everything's smooth and evenly combined.

6. Serve immediately with chips for dipping. If you'd like, you can also keep it heated in a slow cooker on the lowest setting, so it stays smooth and soft.

SMOKING TIPS: Mesquite will add a big smoky flavor and more color. If you would like a milder taste, use a mix of cherry and hickory.

KNOW YOUR INGREDIENTS: To make this a more substantial dish, add some crumbled cooked bacon or cooked sausage to the cheese mixture. If jalapeños are too hot for your taste, try 2 teaspoons of chipotle powder instead.

Smoked Almonds

SERVES 8

PREP TIME:
10 minutes

SMOKING TIME:
2 hours
30 minutes

TEMPERATURE:
225°F

WOOD:
Hickory

Smoked almonds from a can? Not anymore, my friend! These smoked almonds are a breeze to make. You'll be craving them year-round as a snack or after-dinner treat.

4 tablespoons (½ stick) unsalted butter

2 tablespoons salt

2 teaspoons freshly ground black pepper

2 pounds skin-on almonds

1. Preheat the smoker to 225°F.

2. In a saucepan on the stovetop, melt the butter over medium heat. Stir in the salt and pepper.

3. Place the almonds in a bowl and pour the seasoned melted butter over them. Stir the nuts to coat.

4. With BBQ mitts, lay a sheet of aluminum foil over a cooking rack. Spread the almonds in one layer on the foil. Use more foil, if necessary, to make sure the almonds are in one layer.

5. Set the rack in the smoker and smoke the almonds for 2 hours 30 minutes, stirring the almonds halfway through to make sure they get evenly smoked.

6. Let the almonds rest for 30 minutes before serving.

PAIR IT WITH: These smoked almonds are great with Smoked Cheddar Cheese (page 147).

KNOW YOUR INGREDIENTS: Try smoking pecans for a scrumptious variation.

Smoked Candied Nuts

SERVES 8

PREP TIME:
15 minutes

SMOKING TIME:
3 hours

TEMPERATURE:
225°F

WOOD:
Cherry and
hickory mix

These sweet smoked nuts are a holiday treat that you'll want to make all year round. Indulgent tip: They are as good before dinner as they are after.

½ cup raw almonds

1 cup raw cashews

4½ cups raw hazelnuts

1 cup raw pecans

6 tablespoons unsalted butter

6 tablespoons dark brown sugar

1 teaspoon ground cinnamon

1 teaspoon coarse salt

1 tablespoon dark rum

1. Preheat the smoker to 225°F.

2. Spread the nuts evenly in a shallow baking dish.

3. Smoke the nuts for 1 hour 30 minutes.

4. Take out the pan, stir the nuts around, and return to the smoker for another 1 hour 30 minutes. Check them in the last 30 minutes to make sure they don't get too dark.

5. About 15 minutes before the nuts are done, in a saucepan on the stovetop, melt the butter over medium heat. Stir in the brown sugar, cinnamon, and salt until well combined. Add the rum and keep stirring for 5 to 7 minutes as the mixture thickens.

6. Take the nuts out of the smoker and place them in a bowl. Pour the sugar/butter mixture over them and stir to coat the nuts with the glaze.

7. Serve warm or let cool to room temperature.

KNOW YOUR INGREDIENTS: Be sure to buy the nuts raw, not roasted.

Smoked Bacon-Wrapped Cheese Sandwiches

SERVES 2

PREP TIME:
30 minutes

SMOKING TIME:
1 hour
10 minutes

TEMPERATURE:
250°F

WOOD:
Hickory
or maple

When you bite into the smoky bacon and you taste the spicy, melty cheese, you'll be thinking about making this every day. Is it an appetizer? A meal? No. I'm telling you that this sandwich is an *occasion*.

4 (1-inch-thick) slices bread

6 slices pepper Jack cheese

1 teaspoon cayenne pepper

16 slices bacon

1 tablespoon Pork Rub (page 165)

1. Preheat the smoker to 250°F.

2. Place the bread in the smoker and cook for 10 minutes. This will remove moisture and keep the sandwich from getting soggy. Let the bread cool for 10 minutes.

3. For each sandwich, place 3 slices of cheese between 2 slices of bread. On a sheet of wax paper, arrange 4 slices of bacon side by side, overlapping by about ¼ inch. Set a cheese sandwich on the bacon, 1½ inches in from one of the ends of the bacon. Fold that bacon over the end of the sandwich. With your fingers on the 1½ inch line of bacon, flip the sandwich over, then flip it forward again and the bacon will wrap around one side of the sandwich.

4. Now, to finishing wrapping the sandwich, repeat the arranging of 4 slices of bacon on the wax paper. Set the sandwich over the bacon so that the bacon will wrap the exposed sides and repeat the flipping steps above.

5. Repeat to make the second sandwich.

6. Sprinkle the bacon with the pork rub.

7. Smoke the bacon-wrapped sandwiches for 1 hour, or until the bacon has browned.

8. To serve, cut the sandwiches into quarters.

KNOW YOUR INGREDIENTS: You can use Texas toast instead of normal bread. Just skip the step of drying the bread. Also, feel free to try different types of cheese, or make it spicier by adding slices of pickled jalapeño between the cheese layers. This is a big sandwich; you may want to serve it as a starter for four people.

Smoked Deviled Eggs

SERVES 4

PREP TIME:
50 minutes

SMOKING TIME:
30 minutes

TEMPERATURE:
212°F

WOOD:
Cherry
or hickory

Smoking the eggs after they've been hard-boiled saves a lot of time and the taste is even better and smokier. This is a very easy appetizer that will surprise your family and friends if they haven't tried smoked eggs.

6 large eggs

2 teaspoons salt, divided

2 teaspoons apple cider vinegar, divided

1 teaspoon olive oil

3 tablespoons mayonnaise

2 teaspoons Dijon mustard

1 teaspoon hot sauce

1 teaspoon garlic powder

1 teaspoon onion powder

1 teaspoon freshly ground black pepper

2 teaspoons smoked paprika

1. Preheat the smoker to 212°F.

2. In a medium pot, combine the eggs with enough water to cover by 1 inch. Add 1 teaspoon salt and 1 teaspoon vinegar. Bring to a boil, then reduce to a simmer and cook for 10 minutes. Drain and cool the eggs under cold running water, then peel them.

3. Set the eggs on a grill screen, place in the smoker, and smoke for 30 minutes.

4. Transfer the eggs to a bowl and refrigerate to cool them down, about 30 minutes.

5. Halve the eggs lengthwise. Pop the yolks into a bowl. Place the empty halves of the egg whites on a serving dish.

6. Add the olive oil to the yolks and break them up with a fork until they are well mashed. Add the mayonnaise, mustard, hot sauce, garlic powder, onion powder, pepper, and remaining 1 teaspoon vinegar and 1 teaspoon salt. Blend the ingredients together until they form a thick paste. If you want your deviled eggs to be creamier, add another 1 to 2 teaspoons mayonnaise.

7. Fill each egg white half with about 1 tablespoon of the yolk mixture.

8. Sprinkle the smoked paprika over the filling and serve.

KNOW YOUR INGREDIENTS: These deviled eggs are great when they are even spicier. Feel free to add more hot sauce to the yolk mixture and top them with a pinch of cayenne in addition to the smoked paprika.

Stuffed and Smoked French Toast

SERVES 3

PREP TIME:
15 minutes

SMOKING TIME:
20 to
22 minutes

TEMPERATURE:
275°F
and 350°F

WOOD:
Alder or apple

Here's a sweet way to wow your family and friends on a weekend or holiday morning. The lightly smoke-infused vanilla custard wakes everyone up. You will need a pellet smoker for this. Non-stick grill mats make it an easy recipe!

6 (1-inch-thick) slices egg bread

½ cup whole milk

11 large eggs

1½ teaspoons cinnamon sugar

1 teaspoon pure vanilla extract

8 ounces cream cheese, at room temperature

½ cup canned apple pie filling

½ cup canned blueberry pie filling

½ cup canned cherry pie filling

1 tablespoon powdered sugar

½ cup maple syrup

1. Preheat a pellet smoker to 275°F.

2. Place the slices of bread in the smoker for 10 minutes to dry them out a bit.

3. Increase the temperature to 350°F and place grill mats in the smoker.

4. In a large bowl, mix together the milk and eggs. Add the cinnamon sugar and vanilla and beat the mixture until it's frothy.

5. Spread the cream cheese on one side of each slice of bread. Reserving a little of each pie filling for serving, top 3 of the slices with the pie fillings (one type of filling per slice). Close up the sandwiches, setting the remaining 3 slices on top, cream cheese-side down.

6. Dip each sandwich completely in the egg mixture, letting them soak for about 5 seconds, then immediately place the sandwiches on the grill mat.

7. Smoke them for 5 to 7 minutes, until the bread is browned. Flip the sandwiches and cook for another 5 minutes.

8. To serve, top each sandwich with some of the reserved pie filling and sprinkle with the powdered sugar. Drizzle the maple syrup over it all and serve hot.

PAIR IT WITH: A little Smoked Candied Bacon (page 57) on the side would be a delicious idea!

Basque-Style Cheesecake

SERVES 8

PREP TIME:
20 minutes

SMOKING TIME:
50 minutes

TEMPERATURE:
400°F
and 425°F

WOOD CHIPS:
Maple
or apple

This cheesecake's burnt outside and sweet and creamy inside is a great combination. Use a pellet smoker to get up to the right temperature. I learned that this dessert was invented by the famous chef Santiago Rivera in Spain. With a little smoky flavor, I think the maestro would approve.

1 tablespoon softened butter, for the pan

3 (8-ounce) packages cream cheese, at room temperature

1 cup sugar

½ teaspoon salt

3 tablespoons all-purpose flour

½ teaspoon pure vanilla extract

4 extra-large eggs, at room temperature

1¼ cups heavy (whipping) cream

1. Preheat a pellet smoker to 400°F.

2. Butter a 9-inch cake pan. Cut a sheet of parchment paper large enough to line the bottom and sides of the pan with a few extra inches. Butter the paper and press it into the pan, butter-side up, flattening any major creases. Trim away any excess paper from the sides until you have an inch or two of overhang.

3. In a bowl, combine the cream cheese, sugar, salt, and flour. Stir and smear together with a spatula until very smooth and creamy.

4. Whisk in the vanilla and 1 egg. Add the remaining 3 eggs, whisking each one in completely before adding the next. Pour in the heavy cream and mix until smooth.

5. Pour the batter into the prepared pan. Tap the pan against the counter to burst any air bubbles.

6. Bake the cake in the smoker for 40 minutes.

7. Increase the temperature to 425°F and cook for 10 minutes more, or until it's puffed, well browned, and nearly burned on the edges.

8. Remove the cheesecake and let it cool to room temperature. Lift it out onto a plate and peel back the parchment paper with a spatula. Refrigerate until thoroughly chilled, then serve.

SMOKING TIP: Alder wood is a good choice for an even lighter smoke. You can also try other sweet fruit woods, like cherry or peach, for a bigger smoky taste.

Smoked Pineapple Chocolate Upside-Down Cake

SERVES 8

PREP TIME:
20 minutes

SMOKING TIME:
50 minutes

TEMPERATURE:
350°F

WOOD:
Apple
or maple

This chocolate cake recipe is fun to make as well as delicious. I saved a little time by using a fudge cake mix, but if you have a favorite recipe from Grandma, go for it. She'd probably appreciate your take on her recipe anyway. This recipe requires a pellet smoker.

1 (15.25-ounce) box
double-fudge
chocolate cake mix

⅓ cup vegetable oil

3 large eggs

1¼ cups pineapple juice

⅓ cup unsalted butter

1⅓ cups packed light
brown sugar

7 pineapple rings, canned
or cored fresh

8 maraschino cherries

1. Preheat a pellet smoker to 350°F.

2. Follow the directions on the cake box to make the batter, using the vegetable oil and eggs as directed but substituting the pineapple juice for water.

3. In a 12-inch cast-iron skillet on the stovetop, melt the butter over medium heat. As soon as the butter is melted, sprinkle the brown sugar over it.

4. Set the pineapple rings in the butter and sugar in a circle with one in the middle. Then put one cherry in the center of each ring, pressing them down a little. Pour the cake batter over the pineapple and cherries.

5. Set the skillet on the grill grate in the smoker and smoke for 25 minutes.

6. To make sure it bakes evenly, rotate the pan a half turn and smoke for another 25 minutes. Like all cakes, you'll know it's done when you stick a toothpick or knife blade into it, and it comes out clean.

7. Run a knife around the side of the skillet to loosen the cake. Place a big serving plate or cutting board upside-down on the pan. Then flip everything over to release the cake, but leave the skillet in place. Let the cake rest—with the pan still on top of it—for 5 minutes to set the pineapple and sugar.

8. Remove the skillet and serve the cake warm or cool.

PAIR IT WITH: We're not gonna be mad if you put some ice cream on it!

Chapter 8

Rubs, Marinades, and Sauces

To ADD FLAVOR AND CREATE a tasty crust on smoked food, you need rubs, marinades, and sauces. A dry rub is basically a mixture of herbs, spices, and other dry ingredients that are rubbed onto the surface of a piece of meat, poultry, or fish. Marinades are like brines in the sense that they tenderize meat and help it retain moisture while it's cooking. However, with marinades you can soak the meat for a shorter amount of time than with a brine, while still getting a ton of flavor. Remember to boil the marinade for 5 minutes before using it for basting during the last 20 minutes of smoking. Lastly, winning barbecue is often enhanced by a great sauce. Some of my favorites include my Bacon-Flavored BBQ Sauce (page 170), Spicy Peanut Sauce (page 174), and Chimichurri Sauce (page 171). There are almost as many varieties of marinades, rubs, and sauces as there are people who cook outdoors. So, feel free to try them all and tweak them to your individual liking.

Poultry Rub

MAKES
2½ CUPS

PREP TIME:
10 minutes

This seasoning is for all seasons! It's helpful to have a solid "go-to" dry rub recipe for low-and-slow smoking, roasting, and grilling. This one's mine.

½ cup coarse salt

½ cup smoked paprika

½ cup packed light brown sugar

½ cup minced fresh or granulated garlic

6 tablespoons dried minced or granulated onion

1 tablespoon grated lemon zest

1 tablespoon freshly ground black pepper

1 teaspoon ground cumin

1 teaspoon dried rosemary or oregano

In a medium bowl, mix the salt, paprika, brown sugar, garlic, onion, lemon zest, pepper, cumin, and oregano together. If you use fresh garlic, use the rub within 4 days. With granulated garlic, store in a sealed container for up to 1 month.

KNOW YOUR INGREDIENTS: Make this rub spicy by adding 1 teaspoon of cayenne pepper. For a turkey-specific rub, feel free to add 1 teaspoon of fresh or ground sage.

Pork Rub

MAKES
2½ CUPS

PREP TIME:
10 minutes

It's easy to make your own smoking rubs. This blend is great for ribs, chops, tenderloin, and, of course, for pork shoulder when you're making pulled pork.

½ cup coarse salt

½ cup smoked paprika

½ cup packed light brown sugar

½ cup minced fresh or granulated garlic

6 tablespoons dried minced or granulated onion

2 tablespoons chopped fresh thyme or 2 teaspoons dried thyme

1 tablespoon freshly ground black pepper

½ teaspoon ground nutmeg

In a medium bowl, mix the salt, paprika, brown sugar, garlic, onion, thyme, pepper, and nutmeg together. If you use fresh garlic, use the rub within 4 days. With granulated garlic, store in a sealed container for up to 1 month.

KNOW YOUR INGREDIENTS: Make this rub spicy by adding 1 tablespoon of red pepper flakes. To give the rub a deeper, smokier flavor, add 2 teaspoons of chipotle powder.

Beef Rub

MAKES
2½ CUPS

PREP TIME:
10 minutes

This dry rub is a must for smoked brisket, chuck, or steak.

½ cup coarse smoked salt

½ cup smoked paprika

½ cup packed light brown sugar

½ cup minced fresh or
  granulated garlic

6 tablespoons dried minced
  or granulated onion

1 tablespoon dried oregano

1 tablespoon freshly
  ground black pepper

1 teaspoon ground cumin

In a medium bowl, mix the salt, paprika, brown sugar, garlic, onion, oregano, pepper, and cumin together. If you use fresh garlic, use the rub within 4 days. With granulated garlic, store in a sealed container for up to 1 month.

KNOW YOUR INGREDIENTS: Make this rub spicy by adding 1 tablespoon of red pepper flakes. To give your beef flavor a cowboy would love, add 1 teaspoon each of chipotle and ancho powder.

Fish Rub

MAKES
2½ CUPS

PREP TIME:
10 minutes

The citric taste of the lemon zest gives fish just what it needs to bring out that fresh seafood flavor. This Fish Rub accents fish beautifully, but it works equally well with poultry.

½ cup coarse smoked salt

½ cup smoked paprika

½ cup packed light brown sugar

½ cup minced fresh or granulated garlic

6 tablespoons dried minced or granulated onion

1 tablespoon freshly ground black pepper

1 teaspoon grated lemon zest

1 teaspoon chopped fresh or dried dill

In a medium bowl, mix the salt, paprika, brown sugar, garlic, onion, pepper, lemon zest, and dill together. If you use fresh garlic, use the rub within 4 days. With granulated garlic, store in a sealed container for up to 1 month.

KNOW YOUR INGREDIENTS: Instead of dill, use ½ teaspoon of dried tarragon, an anise-scented herb that goes really well with fish.

Seafood Seasoning

MAKES 1⅓ CUPS

PREP TIME:
10 minutes

A little seasoning goes a long way, so long as you brush some olive oil on the fish before you apply it. For a fattier fish, use more seasoning. This seasoning is also a must for smoked shrimp.

½ cup minced fresh or granulated garlic

¼ cup smoked paprika

3 tablespoons dried minced or granulated onion

3 tablespoons coarse smoked salt

1 tablespoon celery salt

1 tablespoon freshly ground black pepper

1 teaspoon chopped fresh or dried dill

1 teaspoon grated lemon zest

½ teaspoon ground ginger

½ teaspoon mustard powder

In a medium bowl, mix the garlic, paprika, onion, smoked salt, celery salt, pepper, dill, lemon zest, ginger, and mustard powder together. If you use fresh garlic, use the rub within 4 days. With granulated garlic, store in a sealed container for up to 1 month.

SMOKING TIP: When using a seafood seasoning, try smoking with woods like hickory or pecan. They can stand up to a lot of spices without being too strong a smoke.

KNOW YOUR INGREDIENTS: To give this a Mediterranean-inspired flair, add 1 teaspoon of dried oregano and 1 teaspoon of dried rosemary. If you want a spicier rub, add 1 teaspoon of cayenne pepper. Or replace the dill with ½ teaspoon of dried tarragon for a nice hint of anise, which goes really well with seafood.

Basic Marinade with Variations

MAKES 8 CUPS

PREP TIME:
5 minutes

Besides dry rubs, bathing meat in a marinade before cooking adds a lot of flavor. A marinade always has some type of slightly acidic liquid, like citrus, wine, vinegar, or fruit juice. The acid, together with pepper, salt, garlic, oils, and herbs, makes the food tastier and more tender. This marinade makes enough to soak about 12 pounds of protein, with enough extra to boil into a basting sauce.

6 cups dry red wine (about one 750 ml bottle)

½ cup olive oil

1 medium to large onion, diced

¼ cup minced garlic

¼ cup chopped fresh parsley

1 teaspoon smoked salt

1 teaspoon coarsely ground black pepper

Variations (see list below)

In a large bowl, whisk together the wine, oil, onion, garlic, parsley, smoked salt, pepper, and any additional ingredients outlined in the Variations.

FOR BEEF: Add 2 tablespoons chopped fresh rosemary or 2 teaspoons dried.

FOR PORK: Add 2 tablespoons chopped fresh thyme or 2 teaspoons dried.

FOR CHICKEN: Replace the red wine with dry white wine. Add 2 tablespoons chopped fresh rosemary (or 2 teaspoons dried) and 1 teaspoon grated lemon zest.

FOR TURKEY: Add 1 teaspoon rubbed sage.

FOR SEAFOOD: Replace the red wine with dry white wine. Add ¼ cup chopped scallions, 1 tablespoon grated lemon zest, and either 2 tablespoons chopped fresh dill (or 2 teaspoons dried) or ½ teaspoon dried tarragon.

Bacon-Flavored BBQ Sauce

**MAKES ABOUT
2¼ CUPS**

PREP TIME:
15 minutes

SMOKING TIME:
30 minutes

TEMPERATURE:
275°F

WOOD:
Maple
or apple

A good BBQ sauce is a must-have for smoking. By now, it shouldn't surprise you that this version includes bacon.

3 slices bacon

1½ cups ketchup

¼ cup pineapple juice

2 tablespoons light corn syrup

1 teaspoon
  Worcestershire sauce

2 teaspoons chili powder

1 teaspoon ground cumin

¼ teaspoon salt

¼ teaspoon freshly
  ground black pepper

1 tablespoon olive oil

6 tablespoons chopped
  yellow onion

2 teaspoons minced garlic

1. Preheat the smoker to 275°F.

2. Lay the bacon slices on a wire rack or grill screen (or directly on the smoker rack, perpendicular to the grate). Smoke for 30 minutes, or until crisp. When cool enough to handle, cut them into ½-inch pieces.

3. In a bowl, combine the ketchup, pineapple juice, corn syrup, Worcestershire sauce, chili powder, cumin, salt, and pepper.

4. In a large saucepan on the stovetop, heat the oil over medium-high heat. Add the onion and garlic and cook for about 5 minutes, or until the onion is tender.

5. Add the ketchup mixture to the saucepan and bring to a boil. Reduce the heat to low. Cook, stirring occasionally, for about 8 minutes to thicken it slightly. Stir in the bacon pieces.

6. Pour the sauce into the bowl and let cool to room temperature before using.

KNOW YOUR INGREDIENTS: I love this sauce on chicken, beef tenderloin, and burgers. Add 1 tablespoon of maple syrup if you want a sweeter taste.

Chimichurri Sauce

MAKES 1½ CUPS

PREP TIME:
30 minutes

SMOKING TIME:
40 minutes

TEMPERATURE:
250°F

WOOD:
Maple or oak

This sauce originated in Argentina and is used all over Latin America for basting meat. I love to spoon it on steaks, chicken, pork, and sausages, but it also works fabulously as a marinade or salad dressing.

1 large head garlic

½ cup extra-virgin olive oil, plus 3 tablespoons

2 tablespoons red wine vinegar

½ cup finely chopped parsley

¾ teaspoon minced fresh oregano

1 teaspoon coarse salt

½ teaspoon freshly ground black pepper

1. Preheat the smoker to 250°F.

2. Cut the top off the garlic head, set it cut-side up, and drizzle it with 3 tablespoons olive oil.

3. Set the garlic in the smoker on a piece of aluminum foil and smoke for 40 minutes, or until it is soft and brown.

4. When the garlic has cooled enough to handle, squeeze the cloves out of their skins and measure out 2 tablespoons (save any remaining smoked garlic for another use).

5. In a bowl, stir together the remaining ½ cup olive oil, the vinegar, parsley, oregano, salt, pepper, and smoked garlic. Let the chimichurri rest for at least 30 minutes before using. You can store chimichurri in the refrigerator for up to 1 week.

KNOW YOUR INGREDIENTS: If you want it spicier, add 2 small red chiles, chopped, with the seeds removed.

Korean-Style BBQ Sauce

MAKES 4 CUPS

PREP TIME:
20 minutes

SMOKING TIME:
40 minutes

TEMPERATURE:
250°F

WOOD:
Oak

This BBQ sauce, inspired by great Korean outdoor cooking, goes perfectly with any type of pork or beef.

1 large head garlic

3 tablespoons sesame oil, divided

1¼ cups soy sauce

1 tablespoon rice vinegar

1½ cups packed light brown sugar

3 tablespoons gochujang or similar red chili paste

1 tablespoon grated fresh ginger

1 teaspoon coarsely ground black pepper

½ cup plus 2 tablespoons water

2 tablespoons cornstarch

1. Preheat the smoker to 250°F.

2. Cut the top off the garlic head, set it cut-side up, and drizzle it with 2 tablespoons sesame oil.

3. Set the garlic in the smoker on a piece of aluminum foil and smoke for 40 minutes, or until it is soft and brown.

4. When the garlic has cooled enough to handle, squeeze the cloves out of their skins and measure out 2 tablespoons (save any remaining smoked garlic for another use).

5. In a saucepan, combine the smoked garlic, soy sauce, vinegar, remaining 1 tablespoon sesame oil, brown sugar, gochujang, ginger, and black pepper. Mix to blend.

6. Set the saucepan over medium-high heat and bring to a boil.

7. Meanwhile, in a small bowl, stir the water into the cornstarch until it's smooth.

8. As soon as the garlic mixture starts to boil, add the corn-starch slurry, whisking thoroughly. Simmer the sauce for 2 minutes to thicken.

9. Let the sauce cool slightly. Use immediately or store for up to 10 days.

PAIR IT WITH: This sauce is made for Korean-Style Short Ribs (page 80)! It's also delicious on Smoked Pork Chops (page 55), Smoked Spicy Baby Back Ribs (page 56), or 3-2-1 Ribs (page 46).

KNOW YOUR INGREDIENTS: Gochujang is a traditional Korean chili paste and is great if you can find it. If you're wary about chili paste, you can use sriracha, a sweeter hot sauce from Thailand. Also, make sure that the ginger is freshly grated; it makes a big difference in the taste.

Spicy Peanut Sauce

MAKES 3 CUPS

PREP TIME:
30 minutes

SMOKING TIME:
45 minutes

TEMPERATURE:
250°F

WOOD:
Cherry

This is the sauce that makes chicken satay more than basic kebabs. It's also fabulous with pork, over noodles, or as a salad dressing.

1 large head garlic

4 tablespoons sesame oil, divided

⅔ cup raw peanuts

2 tablespoons unsalted butter, melted

1 teaspoon coarse salt

3 scallions, diced

1 tablespoon grated peeled fresh ginger

1 cup water

¼ cup soy sauce

¼ cup distilled white vinegar

3 tablespoons light brown sugar

½ teaspoon red pepper flakes

1. Preheat the smoker to 250°F.

2. Cut the top off the garlic head, set it cut-side up, and drizzle it with 2 tablespoons sesame oil.

3. Set the garlic in the smoker on a piece of aluminum foil and smoke for 40 minutes, until softened and browned. Squeeze the cloves out of their skins and measure out 1 to 2 tablespoons (save any remainder for another use).

4. Meanwhile, in a bowl, toss the peanuts and melted butter together. Sprinkle with the salt and toss again. Place the peanuts in a perforated BBQ skillet or a shallow baking dish and smoke them for 45 minutes, stirring every 15 minutes. Don't let them burn!

5. Take the peanuts out the smoker and let cool for about 20 minutes.

6. Transfer the peanuts to a food processor and process for 4 to 5 minutes, until the peanuts turn into a creamy peanut butter. There should be just a little more than ½ cup.

7. In a skillet on the stovetop, heat the remaining 2 tablespoons sesame oil over medium heat until it's hot but not smoking. Add the smoked garlic, scallions, and ginger and cook, stirring constantly, for 90 seconds.

8. Stir in the water, peanut butter, soy sauce, vinegar, brown sugar, and red pepper flakes. Bring to a simmer, stirring constantly until it's smooth. Let it cool to room temperature before serving.

KNOW YOUR INGREDIENTS: You can replace the red pepper flakes with sriracha for a different kind of spiciness.

VOLUME EQUIVALENTS	U.S. STANDARD	U.S. STANDARD (OUNCES)	METRIC (APPROXIMATE)
LIQUID	2 tablespoons	1 fl. oz.	30 mL
	¼ cup	2 fl. oz.	60 mL
	½ cup	4 fl. oz.	120 mL
	1 cup	8 fl. oz.	240 mL
	1½ cups	12 fl. oz.	355 mL
	2 cups or 1 pint	16 fl. oz.	475 mL
	4 cups or 1 quart	32 fl. oz.	1 L
	1 gallon	128 fl. oz.	4 L
DRY	⅛ teaspoon	–	0.5 mL
	¼ teaspoon	–	1 mL
	½ teaspoon	–	2 mL
	¾ teaspoon	–	4 mL
	1 teaspoon	–	5 mL
	1 tablespoon	–	15 mL
	¼ cup	–	59 mL
	⅓ cup	–	79 mL
	½ cup	–	118 mL
	⅔ cup	–	156 mL
	¾ cup	–	177 mL
	1 cup	–	235 mL
	2 cups or 1 pint	–	475 mL
	3 cups	–	700 mL
	4 cups or 1 quart	–	1 L
	½ gallon	–	2 L
	1 gallon	–	4 L

OVEN TEMPERATURES

FAHRENHEIT	CELSIUS (APPROXIMATE)
250°F	120°C
300°F	150°C
325°F	165°C
350°F	180°C
375°F	190°C
400°F	200°C
425°F	220°C
450°F	230°C

WEIGHT EQUIVALENTS

U.S. STANDARD	METRIC (APPROXIMATE)
½ ounce	15 g
1 ounce	30 g
2 ounces	60 g
4 ounces	115 g
8 ounces	225 g
12 ounces	340 g
16 ounces or 1 pound	455 g

SMOKE TIME CHEAT SHEET

FOOD	SMOKING TEMP	SMOKING TIME	INTERNAL TEMP	WOOD
BEEF				
Brisket	225°F	8 to 10 hours	195°F to 205°F	Oak
Filet mignon	225°F	45 minutes to 1 hour	120°F to 155°F	Oak, pecan
Flank steak	225°F	3 hours	120°F to 155°F	Any
Hamburger	250°F	1 hour	160°F	Oak, mesquite, hickory
Jerky	180°F	3 to 4 hours	Until dry and chewy	Hickory
London broil (top round)	225°F	1½ to 2 hours	120°F to 155°F	Any
Prime rib (7- to 8-pound)	250°F	3½ to 4 hours	120°F to 155°F	Hickory, oak, pecan
Ribs (short plate or chuck)	250°F	8 to 10 hours	205°F	Oak
Rump roast	225°F	3 to 3½ hours	120°F to 155°F	Oak, mesquite
Short ribs	225°F	4 to 5 hours	200°F to 205°F	Oak, mesquite
Sirloin steak kebabs	225°F	40 minutes to 1 hour	120°F to 155°F	Oak, mesquite
Tenderloin	225°F	1 to 1½ hours	120°F to 155°F	Oak, hickory, pecan
Tri-tip	225°F	3 to 4 hours	120°F to 155°F	Oak
POULTRY				
Chicken breasts, tenders, fillets (boneless, skinless)	250°F to 275°F	1½ to 2 hours	165°F	Hickory, mesquite, pecan, cherry, maple
Chicken, cut-up (legs, thighs, breasts)	250°F to 275°F	1½ to 2 hours	165°F	Cherry, pecan, oak, apple, maple, hickory
Chicken wings or drummettes	250°F	2 hours	165°F	Oak, mesquite, hickory

FOOD	SMOKING TEMP	SMOKING TIME	INTERNAL TEMP	WOOD
Chicken (whole, 3- to 4-pound)	250°F	3 to 4 hours	165°F	Cherry, pecan, oak, apple, hickory
Chicken leg quarters	275°F	1½ hours	165°F	Mesquite, apple, cherry
Turkey (whole, 10- to 12-pound)	250°F	4 to 6 hours	165°F	Apple, apricot, cherry, peach
Turkey breast (bone-in, 6- to 7-pound)	250°F	3½ to 4 hours	165°F	Apple, mesquite
Turkey legs	225°F	4 to 5 hours	165°F	Apple

PORK

Baby back ribs	225°F	6 hours	190°F	Hickory
Bacon	275°F	2 hours	Until firm and crispy, as desired	Hickory, maple, apple
Bratwurst	225°F	1½ to 2 hours	160°F	Oak, pecan, hickory
Ham, fully cooked (whole, bone-in, 10- to 12-pound)	275°F	5 hours	140°F	Cherry
Pork shoulder / Boston butt (pulled, 8- to 9-pound)	225°F to 250°F	9 to 10 hours	205°F	Hickory
Pork sausage (ground)	275°F	1½ hours	165°F	Hickory, apple
Pork chops	250°F	1½ hours	160°F	Oak, hickory, apple
Pork loin roast (for slicing and serving)	250°F	2½ to 3 hours	160°F	Oak, apple, hickory
Pork loin roast (for pulling/shredding)	225°F	5 to 6 hours	205°F	Oak, apple

FOOD	SMOKING TEMP	SMOKING TIME	INTERNAL TEMP	WOOD
Pork spare ribs or pork belly	250°F	6 hours	190°F	Mesquite, cherry
Pork tenderloin	225°F	2½ to 3 hours	160°F	Hickory, apple
Whole hog	250°F	12 to 13 hours	185°F Hams 190°F Ribs 195°F to 205°F Shoulders	Hickory

SEAFOOD

FOOD	SMOKING TEMP	SMOKING TIME	INTERNAL TEMP	WOOD
Crab cakes, on cedar planks	275°F	30 to 45 minutes	Until lightly browned	Maple, apple
Fish (cod, halibut, mahi-mahi, red snapper, swordfish)	225°F	1 to 1½ hours	145°F	Alder, apple, cherry, oak
Lobster mac and cheese	275°F	1 hour	Until bubbly	Apple, maple
Lobster tails	225°F	45 minutes to 1 hour	130°F to 140°F	Alder, oak
Oysters, raw and shucked	225°F	1½ to 2 hours	Until firm	Alder, cherry, oak, hickory
Salmon (2- to 3-pound)	200°F	1¼ to 1½ hours	145°F	Alder
Sea scallops	225°F	25 minutes	Until opaque and firm	Cherry, oak
Shrimp skewers	225°F	30 to 45 minutes	Until pink and firm	Mesquite, hickory, pecan

FOOD	SMOKING TEMP	SMOKING TIME	INTERNAL TEMP	WOOD
VEGETABLES				
Jalapeño poppers	250°F	1 to 1½ hours	Until tender	Maple
Onions, thickly sliced	250°F	1½ hours	Until tender	Maple, mesquite, hickory
Pattypan squash	225°F	1 to 1½ hours	Until tender	Maple
Potato wedges	275°F	1½ hours	Until tender	Maple, pecan
Mixed vegetables, chopped	225°F	4 hours	Until tender	Maple
OTHER MEATS				
Bacon-wrapped beef fatty	225°F	2 hours	160°F	Oak
Bison brisket	225°F	4 hours	180°F to 190°F	Mesquite
Bologna chub, fully cooked	225°F	3 to 4 hours	n/a	Mesquite
Duck	250°F	4 hours	165°F	Cherry, pecan
Leg of lamb	225°F	4 to 5 hours	145°F	Apple, cherry
Quail	225°F	1 hour	145°F	Hickory
Veal chops	225°F	2½ to 3 hours	160°F	Oak
MISCELLANEOUS				
Nuts	225°F	1 hour	Until dry	Hickory, mesquite

RESOURCES

Alfaro, Daniel. "Learn Where the Cuts of Beef Come From." (The Spruce Eats)
TheSpruceEats.com/cuts-of-beef-chuck-loin-rib-brisket-and-more-995304
This guide explains the qualities of and best ways to cook all cuts of beef.

Beckett, Fiona. "Wine with Food."
MatchingFoodandWine.com/content/wine_with_food
This blog helps you pair wines with all kinds of food.

Fire Food Chef (website). "2021's Best Electric Smoker Reviews & Buying Guide."
FireFoodChef.com/best-electric-smoker-reviews
Most of the "best" electric smoker brands from 2020 still make the best list in 2021. There are some new models and a couple new manufacturers to check out.

Grilla Grills (website). "Pork Cuts: The Ultimate Grilling Guide."
GrillaGrills.com/pork-cuts-for-bbq
Grilla Grills, a manufacturer, has an informative and quick-to-read guide on the best cuts of pork for BBQ. The list includes some of the usual suspects and a few that you may not have considered before.

Hayneedle (website). "Beer & Wine That Pair with Smoked Food."
Hayneedle.com/tips-and-ideas/pairing-beer-wine-smoked-food
There are a lot of pairing options, even within a specific type of smoked food.

The Meatwave (website). "Barbecue Sauce Reviews."
Meatwave.com/reviews
For a guide to bottled BBQ sauces, the Meatwave can't be beat. It presents reviews of nearly 300 sauces.

Online Grill (website). "7 Best Cuts of Beef to Smoke."
TheOnlineGrill.com/best-cuts-of-beef-to-smoke
This guide to seven of the top cuts of beef for smoking and BBQ has information about how to cook these cuts.

Polonski, Adam. "The Best Whiskies for Grilling Season." (Whisky Advocate)
WhiskyAdvocate.com/the-best-whiskies-for-grilling-barbecue
This guide from the Whisky Advocate reviews whiskies that go well with BBQ and grilling.

Seiler, Matthew. "Top 2020 Best Electric Smokers Reviewed—A Complete Buyer's Guide." (Cookout Pal)
CookoutPal.com/best-electric-smokers-reviews
This review of 10 great electric smokers in 2020 is a worthwhile reference with clear descriptions and honest pros and cons.

Shahin, Jim. "Free Range on Food" (Washington Post)
WashingtonPost.com/people/jim-shahin
I started reading stories by Jim Shahin years ago. Now he writes about smoking and BBQ. It's like listening to a friend.

Smoked BBQ (website). "The Best Pellet Smokers for 2021."
SmokedBBQSource.com/best-pellet-smokers
Pellet smokers offer a level of versatility that goes beyond that of "chest-style" electric smokers. This is a good guide to a lot of models on the market today. Fair evaluations help you make your choice.

Wrangham, Richard. *Catching Fire: How Cooking Made Us Human.* (Basic Books, 2009)
If you want to know why we love BBQ and outdoor cooking, this is the book for you.

Zielinsky, Tyler. "How to Pair Any Bourbon with Food." (Whisky Advocate)
WhiskyAdvocate.com/pair-bourbon-with-food
Here's a brief guide on the Whisky Advocate website for pairing bourbon with smoked meals and all kinds of food.

INDEX

MARC GILL is one of the most recognizable Grilling and Kitchen TV "pitchmen." His hectic schedule has him reviewing, testing, and scripting presentations for products sent to him from all over the globe. These products are used in infomercials and other commercial spots and are featured on live shopping TV channels. For the last few years, Marc has been going unplugged at home, doing what he loves most: cooking and feeding family and friends. That's barbecuing, smoking, grilling, braising, and sous vide. On his channel, Marc's on the Grill, he takes his friends into his backyard, where he attempts feats of strength (in cooking), smokes and grills everyone's favorites, and tries out new equipment, accessories, and recipes. For the past 15 years, he has lived in sunny Florida, where he can be found cooking outdoors all year long.

CPSIA information can be obtained
at www.ICGtesting.com
Printed in the USA
JSHW010025150621
15907JS00004B/86